WHEN BEING JEWISH
WAS A CRIME

WHEN BEING JEWISH WAS A CRIME

by
Rachmiel Frydland

THOMAS NELSON INC., PUBLISHERS
Nashville

Scripture quotations are from the
King James Version of the Bible.

Published in Nashville, Tennessee, by Thomas Nelson, Inc.,
publishers and distributed in Canada by Lawson Falle, Ltd.,
Cambridge, Ontario.

Printed in the United States of America.

Fourth Printing

Library of Congress Cataloging in Publication Data

Frydland, Rachmiel.
  When being Jewish was a crime.

  1. Frydland, Rachmiel. 2. Jews in Poland—Biography. 3. Holocaust,
Jewish (1939-1945)—Personal narratives. 4. Converts from Judaism—
Biography. 5. Poland—Biography. I. Title.
DS135.P63F783   940.53'1503'924 [B]   78-16689
ISBN 0-8407-5659-3

Contents

Preface

This book is dedicated to the memory of my parents, my grandmother, and four sisters who, because they were Jews, perished at the hands of the Nazis in various cruel ways during World War II.

It is also sacred to the memory of the hundreds of Hebrew Christians who died in a similar way all over Europe, "the latchet of whose shoes I am not worthy to unloose." They now rest from their labors and enjoy the presence of their Messiah whom they loved more than their own lives.

My prayer is that this book may be a challenge to my own people, the Jews, to consider the claims of the Lord Jesus the Messiah "of whom Moses and the prophets did write."

May it also cause Christians to realize that we are our brothers' keepers, and that God has appointed us to be watchmen for one another—and especially for Israel. May God help us in the days ahead to take a stand and to obey the commands of love of the Lord Jesus, whatever the cost may be.

I want to express my gratitude to all the people who helped with the publication of this book by reading and correcting the English ... and my thanks to those who encouraged me to complete the work.

"The Lord recompense thy work, and a full reward be given thee of the Lord God of Israel, under whose wings thou art come to trust" (Ruth 2:12).

Rachmiel Frydland

Introduction

That Rachmiel Frydland is alive is a miracle. His one-of-a-kind story may not matter to a great many people, but to the large number of those who have received the Lord Jesus through his lengthy ministry, it will mean eternal life.

This man truly walked through the valley of the shadow of death. The worst place a man could be in World War II was in central Europe, and the worst country in Europe was Poland; the worst religion a man could have was Judaism, and perhaps the worst form of Judaism—Hebrew Christianity. Rachmiel Frydland was almost a man alone against World War II. He wandered for years through burning Poland, dazed, bewildered, but always spared. He infiltrated *into* the Warsaw ghetto at a time when Jewish people were trying to tunnel their way out. He challenged the Gestapo face to face. He ran through hails of bullets.

And yet here was a simple and humble man, seeking only to serve his Messiah; quite willing to die, if that were God's will. He was no soldier, surely, but men have been valorously decorated for accomplishing less on the battlefield. He thought of himself as no sort of special saint, but no more sincere a believer was ever denied a seat in church. He is worthy of much praise, but he prefers to receive it only from the Lord when the time of their meeting comes.

Rachmiel Frydland does not have to be an experienced writer of English. His heart cries forth in each sentence. There is a kind of writing that surpasses all considerations of grammar, syntax, and style. It's writing that flows like blood from the veins of the truly worthy. The reader may wonder why there are so many Jewish customs explained. They need to be known because they were an organic part of the life of Rachmiel Frydland. Why are there so many names of people we readers could never know? Because they were heroes, doomed to early deaths but all still living in the heart of Rachmiel Frydland.

I can say only that I am envious of the reader who is about to turn this page. I wish I could again hear this story for the first time.

Zola Levitt

WHEN BEING JEWISH
WAS A CRIME

1

A SABBATH JOURNEY

I was born "before Passover in 1919," according to my father's recollection. The people who were used to utilizing the Jewish calendar, as was my family, did not keep careful track of the Gentile dates, and so I am not able at this time to tell you my birth date.

World War I had ended in 1918 and most of eastern Europe was being established into independent republics. Poland had broken away from the Russian empire, which had two years earlier undergone the Communist Revolution. Germany was being established as the Weimar Republic under the direction of the Social Democratic party. A spirit of nationalism, perhaps stronger in Poland than elsewhere, was growing among the large landowners who were suspicious of both the communism of Russia and the democracy of the United States. Thus, the groundwork was being laid for what later became known as fascism.

My family and I lived in Lesniczowka (meaning "the little forest village"), situated about nine miles west of the river Bug and four miles southeast of Chelm in the Lublin district of Poland. Because our orthodox Judaism discouraged political activity, we were generally unconcerned about the events in our own country much less in someone else's. Besides, we were poor and much of our time was taken up with survival.

My earliest childhood memory concerns a wonderful Sabbath morning when I was about four years old when my father took me to the *minyan*.[1] I remember leaving home speechless with excitement, holding tightly to my father's hand. My mother followed behind us. I carried my father's prayer shawl, the *tallit*, in a special bag. The tallit is a four-cornered garment with fringes attached, to fulfill the commandments of Numbers 15:37–39 and Deuteronomy 22:12; the latter commandment reads: "Thou shalt make thee fringes upon the four quarters of thy vesture. . . ." The tallit was kept in a special bag, in which we also kept the family's handkerchief, because as orthodox Jews we were forbidden to carry anything in our pockets on the Sabbath. This law is in accordance with Jeremiah 17:21: ". . . Take heed to yourselves and bear no burden on the sabbath day." As a minor I was exempt from this law.[2]

Our minyan was held in the home of Reb Eli, the most prosperous Jew in our general territory. Reb Eli's oldest daughter was married to a Cohen, a man who claimed descent from Aaron, the original high priest of Israel. This was important because a Cohen had two privileges: He was the first called to read

---

[1]Minyan: a quorum of ten adult males over the age of thirteen, which is necessary for public prayers.
[2]Minors: according to rabbinic teaching, minors are not punished for the transgression of the ceremonial law up to the age of twelve or thirteen when they become Bar Mitzva, sons of the Law.

the Torah,[3] and it was he who pronounced the sacred Aaronic benediction found in Numbers 6:24–26. A Levite would normally follow the Cohen in the reading of the Torah scroll, but since we did not have a Levite in our minyan, our Cohen was called once again for the second reading. After him, six more readers participated in the assigned weekly portion from the Torah.

We had arrived early that morning, and we were offered coffee and cookies. As a minor, I could eat the cookies before the lengthy morning prayers. My parents declined the cookies, but drank the coffee. They made certain I thanked the host.

I counted the men when we arrived and found only five. Nothing would transpire until five additional men arrived to make up our minyan. Everyone looked out the window from time to time, patiently awaiting the other men traveling from farther away. Soon our friend Moshe arrived with his wife and son; Moshe's son was about sixteen and old enough to qualify for the minyan. And finally Moshe-Yoseph arrived with both his son and son-in-law; those three completed our quorum of ten. Moshe-Yoseph's son-in-law was both *hazan*, the leader in prayer, and *baal koreh*, the one who reads the prescribed weekly section from the Torah with the traditional chant. They also were offered coffee, but Moshe-Yoseph would not drink even coffee before prayers. He was the most pious of all of us, and we had great respect for him.

---

[3]Torah: here the scroll of the Law, the Pentateuch written by a scribe on parchment, but the word has also a wider connotation. It means also all of Jewish tradition.

It was only by a technicality of the Law that we enjoyed the company of the dedicated Moshe-Yoseph. In actual fact, the distance this pious one had to travel to attend our particular prayers exceeded the "legal Sabbath journey" of about a mile from one's home, based on Exodus 16:29, ". . . let no man go out of his place on the seventh day."

Rabbinical logic, however, found a way to extend the Sabbath journey to double the distance. An individual was permitted to have a light meal on Friday at the end of his Sabbath journey at the place where he would stop to rest or spend the night. This place would legally serve as his place of residence and he could therefore travel another mile *from* this specially created "home" where he had had the meal. This practice is called in Hebrew *erub*, the mixing up of homes. Thus Moshe-Yoseph, in effect, had two homes. And thus he could legally journey two miles on the Sabbath.

With the exception of Reb Eli, who owned a turpentine factory, we were all paupers. We peddled produce, which we bought from the farmers and carried to the town of Chelm to sell at a profit and many times at a loss. Occasionally well-to-do merchants would come through town to buy animals from the peasants, but our group were mainly peddlers. My family had a small store established in our home in addition to the peddling we did, and we sold a few essentials to the peasants, such as soap, sugar, matches, hairpins, and hard candy for children. Other Jewish families in their respective villages had such home stores. Moshe-Yoseph had additional income as a glazier (one who cuts and sets glass), and he also owned a few acres of land.

The harder we worked, the poorer we seemed to become. Apart from the fortunate Reb Eli, we simply could not eke out a living. Our customers, for one thing, were too poor to pay us. The peasants would buy from us on credit and then simply omit paying the bills. There was certainly no way for us to collect our accounts, since we were the only Jewish family in a large village. We actually were even afraid to stop the credit.

As a result, we were eventually forced to give up our store, and Moshe-Yoseph had to sell his few acres of land.

Our relations with the non-Jewish population were never very good, but at least the opposition was divided. There were the Polish-speaking Gentiles who were Roman Catholics, some more pious than others. We were most afraid of them. We considered them idol worshipers. My parents were proud to point out to me that they taught their children to consider the images on their walls as gods. There was not a home without at least three images: one of Jesus with His heart showing; one of the *matka boska*, the "mother of God"; and one of Joseph, the husband of Mary. The priest would come to the village at times and bring the "transubstantiated" wafer, which they believed became the flesh and blood of the Messiah. But at that time the priest's coming only hardened our hearts. We knew we worshiped the only true God, and not priests and images.

There were some Russian and Ukrainian peasants who were more friendly. They too were in the minority and treated us better than the Polish-speaking Gentiles did. They were of the Greek Or-

thodox religion, but we did not know the difference
between their religion and that of the Roman
Catholics. They called their priests "popes"; these
priests were married and wore beards, whereas the
Polish priests were unmarried and shaven.

There was another Gentile minority, perhaps
more noticeable to us than the former. They were
the hard-working and prosperous German-speaking
peasants. They called themselves Lutherans or
evangelicals. A revivalist pastor would come to our
village to hold special meetings from time to time,
and these were normally conducted in the home of
the Hubschers, our next-door neighbors. As the
meetings progressed, the Hubschers started to borrow extra chairs from us as they needed them, and
we began to see something rather wonderful happen. The group not only saw to it that the furniture
was returned to us, but a number of them came to
confess their sins to us. One peasant girl, with tears
in her eyes, told us how she had stolen hairpins from
our store, and she wanted to pay for them at whatever price we asked, for she had been converted.
Another man came and told us that he had taken
goods on credit with no intention of paying us, but
he also had been converted and now wanted to pay
his debts. He was not able to pay with money, but he
would pay with produce, eggs, or fruit, for he had no
other means.

Then Mother came home and told us that old Mrs.
Hubscher herself had been converted and that she
now sang the Psalms of David most of the time.
Others came and began to talk, or witness, to my
father about Moses and the Jewish patriarchs. They
were very serious about it, although my father at

first tried to brush them off with light talk. "However," he said, "they are sincere, and they know much about our Torah."

Unfortunately this new spiritual situation didn't seem to last. Except for a small group of three or four families who gradually withdrew from the official Lutheran church to establish their own meetings, the rest of the Hubscher group soon resumed their normal worldly lives. Nevertheless this was a glimpse—a ray of light for us from the God of Israel—to challenge our prejudices toward the Gentiles.

Undoubtedly those simple, honest folk who had come from next door to reveal their hearts to us had made a deep impression on my own heart in those early times. I was unable, of course, to appreciate more fully what moved the despised Gentile to a genuine compassion for his fellow man.

2

"SEND A YESHUA . . ."

Christian worshipers, accustomed to spontaneous prayer, would consider the Jewish prayer regimen of my youth cumbersome and much too highly regulated. It is true that we acted a great deal in accordance with complicated formulas.

Jewish prayer life, though admittedly dedicated and pious, consists largely of reciting prayers from the *siddur*, the Hebrew prayer book. These prayers in Hebrew were composed throughout the centuries by respected Jewish sages.

It was considered natural for us to pray in Hebrew, though this was not our vernacular language. It would have been quite presumptuous, a display of *hutspah* (audacity), to reject the beautifully composed prayers of the siddur in favor of our own prayers. This is not to say that in daily life there were not the normal yearnings of people's hearts expressed in our own language. We might well express in Yiddish, "O God, send a yeshua[1] for the Jewish people. . . . O Lord of the Universe, save us. . . ." However, these were the private exclamations of private people, who would never have

---

[1]Yeshua: salvation, help, the name of Jesus in Hebrew, although we did not realize it.

considered them equal to the formal prayers collected in the siddur. Prayer offered to God could come only from the thick, heavy prayer book, in the exact words in which the venerated rabbis had composed them.

We also had to be aware of the special occasions requiring special prayers. Some of the prayers were to be recited daily, and then there were other special ones for the Sabbath, the High Holy Days, and many other particular occasions. I remember from my childhood the morning prayers, starting with the Modeh Anee, "I thank Thee that Thou hast restored my soul by Thy great compassion according to Thy faithfulness." Then began the long prayers with the *Shema*[2] when we put on the four-cornered small garment, the *tallit katan*, with the fringes, and said: "Blessed be the Lord God who sanctified us and commanded us to have fringes." We repeated in addition to the Shema two more verses, Deuteronomy 33:4 and Proverbs 1:8. In my case, this was considered to be enough for a child.

My father had more arduous prayer tasks to accomplish. Through the week he would study the *sedra*, the six chapters from the Pentateuch to be read in the synagogue the following Sabbath morning, and a corresponding chapter from the prophets called *haftora*. He chanted all of this material twice in Hebrew and once in the Aramaic Targum, a translation ascribed to Onkelos, which rabbinical Judaism considers authoritative. Then he recited part of the prayers for which no minyan was necessary.

[2]Shema: "Hear, O Israel." The verses we recited were Deuteronomy 6:4–9, 11:13–21, and Numbers 15:37–41.

These latter prayers began with the words, "How goodly are thy tents, O Jacob, thy places, O Israel." Then followed a confession of God's unity and an admission of our unworthiness. My father then recited the thirteen principles of Rabbi Ishmael, by which one can study the Torah, and closed with a prayer that the temple in Jerusalem would soon be rebuilt and that this recital be accepted in place of temple sacrifices.

Our public prayers were divided into two halves. The first half, led by Reb Eli's son-in-law, included the reciting of a number of Psalms and were interspersed with various prayers and benedictions. The prayers became more meaningful when Moshe-Yoseph took over the leadership of the second half, which started with the words *Shokhen ad,* "Thou who abidest forever, Holy and Exalted is Thy name."

People who recite formula prayers oftentimes do them quickly and by rote, but Moshe-Yoseph would never speed up. Though everyone by this time of the morning would begin to feel hungry, our cousin would give each prayer its due. Noontime would be on us before he would finish, but we certainly bore him no grudge for his extra measure of devotion. As I think of him now, I realize what a pity it was that Moshe-Yoseph did not know the joy of salvation through the Messiah, as he sought, in his own way, a way of getting into *gan eden,* paradise.

We did breathe a sigh of relief when the prayers finally ended after noontime. We would then take leave of one another with the words *gut shabbes,* "a good Sabbath day," and we would gratefully hurry home to eat.

My home did not offer a great deal of comfort. By today's American standards our poverty would be stupefying. Our little frame house was rectangular and divided into three almost-equal compartments. The roof was steep and always covered with heavy snow in the winter. We lived in two rooms and used the third as a barn. At first, when we still had our cow, we kept her in the barn and Mother was happy that she had enough milk for the children. Father had received the cow as a dowry, together with the house and an acre of land. Later, when business declined and we lost our little "store" and all the money we had, Father decided to sell the cow to finance a little bit of street peddling. Mother wept and begged him not to sell it, for he might lose the money again, and then she would not have milk for the children. Her plea, however, was to no avail, and we sold the cow and bought a few chickens. Father was again in business from the balance of the money.

In the kitchen was a brick oven that we used on Fridays to bake our large pumpernickel bread for the coming week. After the bread was taken out, the oven was reheated and the Cholent[3] was put in. The oven was then sealed, and on the Sabbath day, after we came home from the minyan, we opened the oven and had piping hot food to eat. This procedure was necessary since no cooking was permitted on the Sabbath, in accordance with Exodus 35:3: "Ye shall kindle no fire throughout your habitations upon the sabbath day."

The Jewish year of 5685 came when I was six years

[3]Cholent: a Sabbath day dish of slow-baked meat and potatoes.

old and was an important one for me. This was the year my parents decided to take me with them to the nearby city of Chelm to celebrate the High Holy Days of the Jewish New Year and the Day of Atonement, called in Hebrew respectively *Rosh Hashana* and *Yom Kippur*. Chelm was a mere four miles down the road, but it was an arduous journey in those days, and for me it was a safari of high adventure.

During the month of Elul preceding these holy days my father was more careful than usual in his prayers and in his business. In this month we had congregational prayers even on weekdays. We added an extra recital of Psalm 27 and the sounding daily of the *shofar*, the ram's horn, which was done both to call people to repentance and to remind God of the ram which was sacrificed instead of Isaac (see Gen. 22). I was told that this was a time when even the fish in the sea trembled, for they too were afraid of the judgment of God. It is said in the prayer book: "The great shofar is sounded and a still, small voice is heard. Even the angels in heaven proclaim fearfully and tremblingly, Behold the Day of Judgment."

In effect, Judaism endures a Judgment Day annually on Yom Kippur, and serious worshipers scrupulously prepare for it.

As the old year was drawing to a close, there was even more religious activity. The last week of the old year we arose at midnight, and carrying lanterns, we went to gather ourselves together for special prayers called *selikhot*, as it is written, "At midnight I will rise to give thanks unto thee because of thy righteous judgments" (Ps. 119:62).

The days were shorter now and the rains came

more often. We carried our provisions little by little to Reb Eli's house, for we were to go to town with him and his family for the High Holy Days. We were not overloaded, and the horses were well fed and strong. Reb Eli knew and kept the rabbinical teaching that one was not permitted to eat until his animals were fed.

For me the excitement of it all was overwhelming. I was not only going to visit the "big city" of Chelm for the first time, but in addition, I was to meet my maternal grandmother. It might seem remarkable for a six-year-old child to have never encountered his grandmother who lived so nearby, but this was just another result of our poverty.

I was as good and obedient toward my family as my family was toward God in those days before the High Holy Days. I greatly feared that I might be left behind at the last moment.

The day finally came. I was given a seat right behind the driver, and I felt happy and important. About a mile outside of Chelm the dirt road turned into one made of rounded stones. It was difficult traveling, for the wheels of our wagon were covered with steel, but soon the longed-for town appeared, and the discomforts were forgotten.

Everything in town seemed to be wonderful: the sidewalks where one could walk during and after the rain without getting one's feet muddy; the houses that seemed to be one on top of the other; the water pump where one could get water without always being afraid that the bucket would drop off the hook of the drawing pole and be lost in the depths. Could there possibly be any place in our creation more marvelous than Chelm?

We stayed with Grandmother. She still had two unmarried daughters, who fixed and prepared everything for our arrival. They lived in a rented three-room apartment somewhat below street level. My uncles were no longer at home; two of them lived in Warsaw where they had a drugstore, and the oldest, Shlomo, a physician, was in Moscow. (After the revolution of 1917, he telephoned Grandmother to say that he was alive but could not leave Russia.)

I was careful to note who my relatives were and where they were. How ironic and useless an exercise that was, in the light of what was to happen to all of those people, my family, as these most horrible times for the Jews progressed.

3

THE DAY OF ATONEMENT

These High Holy Days that we were to celebrate actually refer to the Feast of Trumpets and Day of Atonement, as described in Leviticus 23:24–32. The Feast of Trumpets is regarded as the Jewish New Year, and the calendar years move up at that point. The Day of Atonement still maintains its awesome character of confession and repentance, as given in the Scriptures.

Our New Year celebration lasted two days. Then followed seven days of repentance. These nine days, together with the Day of Atonement which immediately followed, are called "The Ten Days of Repentance," or "The Ten Days of Awe, The Ten Fearful Days." It is in these tremulous days that the Jew stands before God, his character open to examination and judgment by the Almighty.

On New Year's Eve my father bought a piece of pineapple, a great delicacy in Poland. He dipped it in honey and gave each of us a bite, reciting this prayer in Hebrew: "May it be Thy will that this be a good and sweet year."

For the evening and morning prayers we went to the synagogue, which was used on weekdays as a *beth-hamidrash*, a house of study of the Torah. The prayers differed little from those I already knew, except that there were more of them and they were more fervent. There was also the repeated sounding of the shofar with the appropriate prayers.

Then came the eve of the Day of Atonement, the most solemn day of the whole year. We began the day with the usual prayers, but this day we also had the *kapores shlogen*.[1] Each female had a hen and each male a rooster. We first had to recite thrice in Hebrew Psalm 107:10, 14–21, and Job 33:23,24. Then the fowl was waved over the head and the following words were said three times in Hebrew: "This is my atonement, this is my ransom, this is offered in exchange for me. This chicken will be put to death, and I will go instead to meet a good, long, and peaceful life."

We carried the chicken to the ritual slaughterer, the *shokhet*, and paid our fee. He took the chicken, pronounced the benediction, tried his slaughter knife, the *halef*, lest it have any indentation (which would make it unfit for ritual slaughtering), and plucked some feathers from the neck in the place where he was going to cut. Then he cut half-way through the neck, stretched the head so that it might bleed a little, pushed out the windpipe to make sure that he cut it through, and threw the chicken on the floor where it bled to death. We went home and Mother plucked the chickens, soaked them in water, salted them, and left them in the salt for an hour so that the rest of the blood could drain out. Only then were they properly prepared to be cooked.

---

[1]Kapores Shlogen: literally, *killing an atonement;* this was probably done to substitute for the goat of Leviticus 16 that carried the sins of Israel.

Eating on the eve of the Day of Atonement, according to rabbinical teaching, is as much an obligation and merit as fasting on the following day; hence the meal was sumptuous and plentiful. After the meal and before sunset there was the kindling of the Holy Day candles. In addition, like others, we placed twenty-four-hour anniversary, or *yahrzeit*, candles in the synagogue in memory of departed loved ones. Mother wept and Father had tears in his eyes as they gave us the traditional blessings on this day; then we departed for prayers at the rabbi's house.

There is some confusion in people's definitions of rabbis, since we encounter such a variety of them today. In my Orthodox Jewish community there were several kinds of rabbis. (Every married man was addressed as Reb, but this did not denote that he was a rabbi.) All teachers were addressed by their pupils as Rabbi. A rabbi ordained and appointed to be the head of a Jewish congregation was known as the Rav; he was rarely referred to by his name. When the Rav was called to read the Torah, he was addressed as *moreh morenu*, teacher of teachers. People typically came to him with the time-honored questions pertaining to the Jewish law, and a well-respected rabbi could anticipate visitors from near and far who would seek his opinions about the perplexing traditions, customs, and statutes of Judaism. There were also rabbis with no congregations who simply became known as leaders through their dependable wisdom and service. They were pious men who gained many orthodox followers.

To distinguish between these untitled rabbis, they were known by the names of their various Polish and Russian towns where they had established their reputations. There were no particular qualifications necessary for this last kind of rabbi except that he have followers, which in Hebrew were called *hassidim* (saints). My father was a follower of the rabbi of Reywitz, and he believed this rabbi could perform mighty miracles.

Indeed, the rabbi had seemed to vindicate this reputation for my father. Before my birth my father lamented that he had four daughters and no one to say *kaddish* over him after his death—the kaddish, or sanctification prayer, is said for eleven months after a death, and on each anniversary, by the son of the deceased. Thus my father went to the marvelous rabbi of Reywitz with the request for a son. It was necessary to give the rabbi a *pidyon*, the so-called "redemption money"—actually, a freewill gift—and, in return, the rabbi would give the seeker a special blessing. Sure enough, soon after my father consulted with the genius of Reywitz, I was conceived.

When I came of age to understand these things, my father took me back to the rabbi to show him the results of his blessing. But because of what transpired on that visit, I was not as impressed with the rabbi of Reywitz as my father was. We waited our turn, gave our pidyon money to the rabbi's treasurer, and received the slip of paper expressing my father's request for an audience with the rabbi. It turned out to be a brief and rather cold interview. The rabbi barely glanced at the paper and gave my father just time enough to introduce me and tell the rabbi that I was the miracle. The rabbi permitted us to touch the tips of his fingers, instead of offering a handshake, murmured a rote blessing, and dismissed us.

In defense of all rabbis, however, it should be said that among their ranks were many men of unquestioned devotion to God and duty. There were decent, pious men—true servants of their fellow man and of the almighty God.

But, let's get back to what occurred on the Day of Atonement. The people crowded into the rabbi's house, and soon the room in which we were to pray became full and stuffy. Each worshiper brought with him a yahrzeit candle, the flame of which was to last for at least twenty-four hours. The prayers dragged along slowly for me, and with the smoke and smell of the candles and the closeness of the crowd, I became sick and faint. It was hardly a healthful atmosphere for a six-year-old boy, and anyway I was not yet responsible for my own atonement. I was not, of course, able to participate fully in the prayers, because I could not read the Hebrew yet, but I did know the names of some of those magnificent prayers. My father perceived my discomfort and finally gave me permission to leave the prayer room and go out to the corridor in the rabbi's house.

But I had experienced some of the great and mighty prayers of Judaism. There was the *Kol Nidra* prayer, in which we asked God that:

> . . . all vows, prohibitions, oaths, vows of dedication, of abstinence and of promises to pay fines: that we may vow or swear, dedicate to and impose a prohibition upon ourselves; even from this Yom Kippur and until

the Yom Kippur that is to come upon us and upon all Israel (with happiness) I do regret them all, let them all be absolved, each one of them. . . . Our vows are no more vows, our prohibitions are nonexistent, and our oaths are no more oaths.

It is said that this Aramaic prayer was composed during the Spanish Inquisition, when Jews under duress promised to accept Roman Catholic "Christianity." Naturally some of them later recanted this oath. Thus, by this Kol Nidra prayer, the Jews had an escape clause, in case of anything similar happening to them in the coming year. It is possible, however, that the prayer may have an earlier origin. The Inquisitors were hardly the first to exact unwilling vows from the mouths of persecuted Jews.

There was also the *Al-Khet* prayer repeated several times during that holy day. It is a recital of all possible sins that are in existence that we may have sinned willingly or unknowingly. Truly, the Scriptures call for a twenty-four hour confessional on this singular Day of Atonement (see Lev. 23:32).

In Orthodox synagogues the evening prayers on this special day are preceded by the prayer of purification, *Tephilah Zakkah*, a long prayer in which we say, among other things:

We are approaching Thee with a broken and crushed heart as poor and needy and unworthy ones to ask for pardon, forgiveness, and atonement on all of the things that we have sinned and transgressed before Thee. O God, we know our evil and the sins of our fathers. We are ashamed and dare not lift up our faces before Thee, like a thief is ashamed when he is found out. How dare we open our mouth and lift up our heads when by our many sins we have caused that the holy image of God should pass away from us, that image which Thou hast placed upon us so that neither the evil one, nor any accuser, should be able to harm us, as it is written: "And all the people of the earth will see that the name of the Lord is written upon you and they shall be afraid of you." We changed it to the unclean image and we have dressed ourselves in unclean garments. . . .

And may it happen that, by the diminishing of our fat and blood as a result of the fast, we may have an atonement for all that we have sinned, that we have done evil and that we have transgressed before Thee. Mayest Thou consider this our fast as though we would have offered a sacrifice of our own bodies upon the altar, and that it may be received by Thee, a sweet-smelling savor, as a sacrifice and burnt offering.

It was quite late at night when we arrived home, and we retired after reciting the Shema. The big meal we had enjoyed before the coming fast and the crowded prayer house had made us thirsty, but we could not have water. On this special day even little children have to fast at least part of the time.

The next morning we went again to the rabbi's house for prayer. I was astonished to see that a number of people who had spent the night were still at their prayers. Through the night they had recited the Psalms and studied the Talmud, particularly the description of the Day of Atonement *(tractate Yoma)*, as it was practiced back in the Jerusalem temple.

If my endurance had been brief on the previous night, it was even worse this morning. The air was even heavier with the candles still burning and the worshipers still crowded together in their murmurings. I had had no breakfast and was in no condition to withstand the marathon prayer session. At around 11:00 my father glanced at me and realized that my time had come. He slipped me a sandwich and told me to eat it outside.

Everyone was certainly relieved when it came to the *Ne'ilah* prayer (that is, the prayer before the gates of heaven are supposedly locked up). At this time we prayed,

> Since we have no advocate, a mediator to oppose the accuser, mayest Thou declare to Jacob the law and the judgment, and justify us in judgment, oh, Thou, King of justice.

We also implored God by prayers and by the sounding of the shofar to remember Isaac and the ram that was offered in his place. We prayed,

> Open for us the Gate, at the time of shutting the Gate [of heaven] for the day is already declining.

Within this prayer we made our final confession by reciting the Shema, "Hear, O Israel, the Lord our God, the Lord is One." Then we would repeat seven times the words, "The Lord He is God." The shofar was then sounded and the communal wish pronounced, "Next Year in Jerusalem." Thus Yom Kippur came to a close.

The evening prayer, *Maariv*, that followed after sundown, belonged to the following day. It was recited in the greatest haste, for all were hungry. Everyone hurriedly wished one another "a good signature," for it was believed that our fate was written down on Rosh Hashana, and God placed His signature to it on Yom Kippur. American Jewish people continue to wish each other "May you be inscribed," with reference to God's Book of Life. After the Maariv prayer, we hurried home to have our meal, and we were obliged to rush with our meal as well, because Reb Eli was to take us home the same night.

Readers who know the Bible will by this time want to raise many questions about the worship I have explained. Among the most certain to be asked are the following:

1. How did it happen that such sincere Jewish people, who understood their prayers and knew the Word of God, could be satisfied with formality and substitutes like the ram's horn or the chicken for an atonement?

2. Why did we not notice that at the time of sounding the shofar we implored God to accept it in the name of Yeshua (apparently Jesus), "the Prince of the Face of God"? (The name Yeshua appears in the Machsor,[2] and is pronounced at Rosh Hashana.)

3. Why were we so prejudiced against Trinitarian doctrines when we ourselves recited before each important prayer and religious deed the words, "Behold, I am prepared now to praise and adore my Creator, to fulfill His commandment, in the name of the Holy Unity, blessed be He, and His Shekinah, through the One who is hidden and concealed"?

---

[2]Machsor: prescribed prayers for special times of the year.

4. In the Yom Kippur prayer we also recite that unusual acrostic prayer based on Isaiah 53. Here is how it appears in translation:

> Messiah our righteousness has turned away from us. We are horror-stricken and there is no one to justify us. He carried on Himself our sins and the burden of our transgressions, and He was wounded for our transgressions. He loaded our sins on His shoulders, in order to find forgiveness for our iniquities. With His stripes we are healed. O, Eternal God, hasten to create Him for us anew. Make Him to ascend to us from the Circle, bring Him to us from *Seir* to proclaim it to us again, a second time by the hand of Messiah *Yinon*.

Why were we unable to notice that all of the above, plus so much of our other worship, was fulfilled in the New Covenant and in the Lord Jesus? Of course, it is simpler with hindsight to compare the prayers against their fulfillments, but how was it that serious scholars of God's Word, undeniably committed to repentance and the gaining of atonement, did not dream that it was freely available? There is no easy answer, but the following points should be considered:

1. We were prejudiced against Jesus of Nazareth. We never thought of Him as having any religious relationship to us as Jewish people. As we lived in a Roman Catholic country, He became to us the God of the Gentiles, whom *they* worshiped, just as they worshiped a "Mother of God," the saints, the crosses, and the images.

2. It must be appreciated that all of us began reciting these prayers in our childhood, before we even knew what we were saying, so that later on, when we could translate the Hebrew, they were still merely formulas to us. We said our statements by rote, not considering their meanings—rather in the manner that people sing their national anthem or pledge allegiance to their flag. We did not regard the exact content of our prayers as being so important as merely pronouncing them.

3. How were we to know when there was no one to explain these things to us? Later, when some of us had the privilege of meeting the missionary who pointed out the truth to us, our hearts were closed because of so many years of hardening. There was also the fear of taking a stand against the rabbis and the majority of the Jews, and the fear of ceasing to be a Jew, God forbid, as a result of acknowledging the Lord Jesus as the Messiah. Jewish people who believed in the Messiah were, at the beginning, regarded as having given up Judaism, as they are even today.

In spite of all these factors, we are amazed at the testimony of history that in all generations there have been Jews, and even rabbis, who overcame all prejudices and received the Lord Jesus and tried to share the knowledge of Him with others. To me, brought up with all the prejudices against Christianity, this is a sheer miracle, and it is a new proof that He is the only Savior, Messiah, and Lord.

4

BREAD FROM
THE EARTH

I remember welcoming the following springtime at the Festival of Purim. The snow began to melt, and the storks came back from the distant countries to their homesteads. The fields were soon covered with green.

On the fourteenth day of the month of Adar we celebrated Purim. The festival was in memory of the fall of Haman, who wanted to destroy the Jewish people, and Mordecai and Queen Esther, who averted the disaster. Without the courage of Esther and the events recorded in the Old Testament book given her name, the world would not have the Jewish people nor their Scriptures.

After Purim we began preparations for Passover. That year the few Jewish families decided to bake the unleavened cakes, the *matzos*, by themselves, rather than buy them ready-made in town. Our house was chosen to be the place where the matzos would be baked. Great care was taken lest there be anything leavened around the house (a grain of wheat, or rye, a crumb of bread), for then all the labor would be in vain. Everything was done quickly, and we all helped.

For the Jew, Passover is somewhat like Christmas

for the Christian, for it is also a special time for children. The older people did not enjoy eating the hard and dry passover cakes, the matzos, for eight full days, but the children reveled in it. My father also prepared the wine all by himself and he gave us the squeezed-out raisins, a delicacy in eastern Europe where there were no vineyards.

I was able to participate in the Passover rituals by chanting these four questions (the questions translate as statements):

> Why is this night different than any other night? All other nights we may eat both leavened and unleavened food, but this night only unleavened. All other nights we eat various herbs, but this night we eat only bitter herbs. All other nights we do not dip one food in the other, but this night we dip our food twice. All other nights we eat our food in a regular manner, but this night we are leaning on cushions.

This gave my father, the head of the house, the opportunity to begin chanting in the Hebrew language the overwhelming story of the exodus from Egypt and to perform the various symbols having to do with the redemption from bondage and the final salvation through Messiah.

Again I was active in the ceremony by attempting to steal the piece of hidden matzo called *afikomen*. Before the Passover ceremony began my father took the special bag in which three matzos had been placed. Taking out the middle matzo, he broke it in two and hid the larger piece. We were not supposed to know where he had hidden it, and later one of my sisters or I would find the piece and demand a gift for it. This piece was important because the Passover service would not be complete without dividing the afikomen and passing a piece of it to every member of the household. This was a substitute for the *Pesah*[1] sacrifice in which all the members of the house had to participate.

Many Christians today realize the deep significance of Passover, from which is taken the Lord's Supper. It was only many years later that I began to see that the three matzos represented the Trinity, and that it was the middle one, the Son, which was broken for us. I watched my father solemnly wrap it in white linen, "bury" it, and then bring it out again—resurrected—at the time of the *third* cup of wine. Truly the Lord had said that this piece of pure, unleavened, and broken bread was His body. We all partook of it at the Passover table along with the third cup, which we called the Cup of Redemption. Even in the Jewish blessing over bread was hidden a beautiful prophecy of the Resurrection. My father would pronounce this blessing, just as Jesus had pronounced it centuries earlier.

> Blessed art Thou, O Lord our God, King of the Universe, who bringest forth bread from the earth.

Soon after Passover the day came when Father took me to a little town called Ruda-Huta, where there was a large Jewish community of about a hundred families. There was a genuine synagogue there and a full-time rabbi, whose main income came from selling candles for the Sabbath lights.

[1]Pesah: passover

The community also had two ritual slaughterers of animals (called *shokhets*) and three teachers for the Jewish children (called rabbis by us, but the older people referred to them as *melameds,* instructors). I was to be enrolled as a student of one of these teachers, and thus began my varied school career.

You see, ever since I had reached school age, the public school teacher in our village had come to our home often and insisted that I attend school. My father kept finding excuses, for he did not want his only son to be contaminated by non-Jewish studies. The teacher was insistent because some of the peasants were saying it was unfair that their children, who could be useful on the farm, had to attend school while the Jewish children remained at home.

This year my father had given in, and I attended public school for two days just before Passover. But after enrolling me in school in Ruda-Huta, my father claimed that I was going to the public school in that town, but actually the public school there did not know I existed. Thus my father, like most religious Jews in Poland, got around the Polish government's public school attendance laws so that his son could concentrate on the Torah.

I was only eight years old when we set out for our journey. This was my first long walk, and so we had to have two main rest stops on the way: one at the home of a Polish farmer whom my father knew, and another at the home of a Jewish farmer less than a mile from our destination. In our subsequent walks from our home to my school in Ruda-Huta, we often stopped to rest at these homes, and I came to know our neighbors better. The Polish family, of whom my father and others spoke so reverently, was named Waldowski. He was called "The American" and was the richest peasant farmer in the neighborhood. In his youth he had gone to the United States, worked on farms, and saved money; then he came back to Poland and bought two of the largest farms. He often boasted of his lands and his cows and pigs, but especially of his children who could speak English. Once, as we were leaving his home, my father told me that Mr. Waldowski had an authentic Bible, and that he read from it and knew everything that was going to happen in the future. How I wish that at that time I had asked more about this Bible!

Here I should also add that at the time of the great persecution under Hitler, Mr. Waldowski was the only one in the village who sincerely tried to help us and another Jewish family by giving us food and employment as long as he was able.

At the home of the Jewish family we had tea and cookies. We spent a long time with them, as Father liked to tell about our home, his business, and the children. I was pleased to hear my father praising me before other people.

After arriving in Ruda-Huta we went to the home of Reb Gershon, the most famous melamed in town. But because his *heder*, or school, was already full, he would not accept me. He sympathized with my father but could not help since, besides teaching me, he would have to keep me in his house the whole week and the teacher's wife, the *rebbetzen*, would have to cook for me and find me a place to sleep in their home.

Another teacher, Reb Pinhos, agreed to receive me into his heder. He had a good name as a teacher, but he often fought with his wife, and many times he ran away from her. Therefore, he did not have many students and had to take the ones who could not get into Reb Gershon's heder. Not long after I started school there the teacher again fought with his wife and ran away, giving us an unexpected vacation. How we loved it!

But, of course, Reb Pinhos eventually returned to his responsibilities. I was put in the advanced class, for I could already read Hebrew, which my father had taught me at home. Our studies consisted of the fluent reading in Hebrew of the prayers and psalms, and the rabbi-teacher corrected any mispronounced word. Later we studied *Humesh*, the Pentateuch in Hebrew, with the teacher pronouncing and translating each word into Yiddish as the pupils repeated after him in unison. As we advanced in learning, the way of teaching changed. The teacher then read for us full sentences of the commentaries and explained their meaning. For the more advanced he explained full paragraphs, chapters, and divisions.

For us the symbol of the teacher was his whip, which he always carried. He would whip us hard or lightly over our shoulders, depending upon the gravity of our error, and he kept his whip busy most of the time.

I did not long for home, as I had better food in Ruda-Huta and Jewish companions to play with after school. Of course, we were sometimes attacked by the non-Jewish boys. Together we watched lest they lay in wait for us as we approached. We hated the Gentile boys, cursed them, and called them *shekotzim*, unclean ones. Sometimes we climbed upon the moss-grown roof of an uninhabited house where we then had a wide panorama of the surrounding area, of houses, meadows, grain fields, and green trees. We would tell stories of what was going to happen when Messiah came. We would dream of participating in the great banquet when the great wild ox, called *shor habor*, who can eat a thousand hills of grass, would be slaughtered for food, together with the great fish, leviathan, who can encircle the whole earth and still put his tail into his mouth. Then there is prepared the specially kept wine from the first six days of creation. All this and much more we talked about as being reserved for us and not for the infidels, the *goyim*.

Sometimes questions came into my mind: Will I be one of the righteous ones? Will I be worthy? It did not bother me at that time because I was under thirteen, and even if I sinned, my father was responsible and would be punished by God for my sins. However, as intensely as the teachers tried to inculcate in us the fear of God, of one thing I was sure: whatever my position in the life to come, it would be far superior, and the punishment far less, than that of the non-Jews. They had no hope whatever, but would suffer eternally and be jealous of our position and privileges as Jews.

The next time Reb Pinhos ran away from his wife, he meant business. He never returned. My father found out about it and came to arrange for my further education.

The heders were all full, but there was one teacher who was willing to accept me. This teacher did not have a great reputation for his ability to teach. As a matter of fact, he had only seven or eight pupils, while other teachers had forty or more. However, he exceeded all of them in piety.

His name was Reb Froyim. He was young, newly married, and his face was emaciated from much fasting. He lived with his in-laws who had several daughters besides his wife, and who had probably promised him food and lodging for the rest of his life. Then, maybe realizing that he would be serving God better by taking in these few pupils who were left without a rabbi-teacher, he took up teaching.

He had no whip, and we knew that he would not hit us; yet we behaved. When we arrived at school, he would still be reciting slowly the morning prayer, still wrapped in his fringed prayer shawl; the large *yarmulke*, or skull cap, was on his head; the phylacteries were bound on his left arm, opposite the heart, and on his forehead; the large girdle divided the upper part of his body from the lower part; and he moved his body backward and forward to avoid any distraction. Mondays and Thursdays he fasted, but on other days he ate some food after prayer. He washed his hands, blessing God for the rabbinical commandment of hand washing; recited Psalm 23; made another blessing, the *hamotsi*, thanking God for bringing forth bread from the earth; dipped the bread in salt and tasted the food. Then he pushed it aside as if it were an evil which one has to partake of for the sake of the good that it might bring. That was another chance to wash his hands and bless God for the food and the goodly land He had given to our fathers. He also prayed for the restoration of Jerusalem and the coming of the Messiah. Then, finally, he was ready to start teaching.

Dear Reb Froyim was not interested in teaching, nor were we pupils interested in learning. We had mutual compassion for one another and so we quickly separated: he to his prayers and mystical studies, and we to our play in the streets. Yet we continued to admire his great piety. In our childish imagination we wondered if he was one of those thirty-six just ones who, according to talmudic legend, uphold the very existence of the world. These just ones were known to God alone and were so important that if they ceased to exist, the world would immediately be destroyed.

The school semester ended quickly. My life was much enriched with experiences and imaginations, although I did not learn very much. However, the adults were not satisfied with Reb Froyim, and the following semester he went out of business. This time my father had begun early negotiations with Reb Berele. He was nicknamed *Kashemacher* because of his additional occupation. At night after teaching, he opened his handmill and turned the buckwheat of the peasants into *kashe*, or groats. This had been his occupation for many years, but he then saw the opportunity of having the more respectable occupation of teaching as well. He would not, of course, refuse the peasant's requests for milling their buckwheat to earn extra money. My cousin and I were his boarders. We were glad to take turns in moving the pole and millstone and watch the buckwheat become something edible. Because of his late nights Reb Berele often fell asleep while a student was reciting, but he was a good teacher and did not use the whip much. He was not as religious as some teachers, and he taught us some arithmetic, the Latin alphabet, and how to read and write the Polish language.

Secularism was in the air, and Reb Berele took note of it.

5

JESUS JUDGED

In these early years I had few contacts of any sort with Christianity. At about this time I learned the stories of Jesus from the Jewish point of view. They are given in the infamous book of legends composed in the Middle Ages and entitled *Toledot Yeshu (The History of Jesus)*. Some of the material is already embodied in the Talmud: that Jesus was born an illegitimate child and He forced Mary His mother to admit it; how He learned sorcery in Egypt; how He made Himself fly up into the sky by sewing the ineffable name of Jehovah into the skin of his leg, but a famous rabbi did the same and brought Jesus down!

A happier memory was the inscription on a Lutheran church that contained a text from Isaiah 56:7, which we recited daily in our prayers: "For my house shall be called a house of prayer for all peoples." I wondered why they should have a text from our prophets? Until now I was under the impression that the Gentiles, the *goyim*, could have nothing to do with our religion and our prophets. Now as I recited my prayers in Hebrew, I was reminded that the text "for all peoples" was not only for us Jews.

One time when my father took me to visit my uncle and aunt, the parents of my cousin with whom I studied, he pointed out to me a humble house and told me that the people who came together there for worship did not hate the Jews. They read our Scriptures and did not have images or crosses on the walls. They were honest and did no one any wrong. (What a joy it was later to have fellowship with these brethren. Even today we continue to keep in touch!)

Probably the happiest days of my life in rabbinical Judaism were those preteen-age years. My teachers liked me and my parents were proud of me.

However, the increasing poverty in my parents' affairs made it impossible for me to return to the school in Ruda-Huta, for my parents could not afford the payments for school and board. So when I was nine years old I went with my parents to spend the High Holy Days in Chelm and there I remained, not in a private school, but in a *yeshiva*, a rabbinical school. The yeshiva was supported by the freewill gifts of the people of Chelm. The parents of the children paid only a token fee and poor students had free tuition and food. Each student was given a list of seven or eight Jewish families and he was to ask them if they would be willing to give him food for one day in each week. My parents had some friends and distant relatives in town who gladly offered to provide my food. Thus I did not need much help from the yeshiva. My mother's cousin offered me food each Sabbath and finally agreed to let me stay overnight while at school, sleeping on a straw sack at night and removing it in the morning. They had three children and a fourth was on the way. A grandmother also stayed with them, and so the apartment was crowded. We all appreciated their consent to take me under such conditions.

There was a certain pride and excitement in being accepted to study at the yeshiva. I was to live in a town instead of a village. But in my memory the change is connected with misery. I did not like sleeping on the floor while all the other members of the family slept in beds. The straw sack on which I slept was put outside during the day, and when I brought it in at night, it was frozen, and it took a long time until it was warmed. My relatives sympathized with me and admired my endurance for the sake of the Torah. The "eating of days," as we called our daily schedule of eating at various homes, was not always pleasant. We had to be at school at a set time and were punished for being late or for not knowing the lecture. How could I explain this to these people who were just getting out of bed in the morning? They would feel insulted if I did not wait a few minutes until they had breakfast fixed for me.

During the semester some of the people who provided the "days" for me went on vacation. New students were arriving, many more aggressive and older than I, and more capable of finding "days." There were days when I was without food, and this began my religious downfall.

One boy in school made money by selling candies which he bought wholesale. I was encouraged to try it. At first I bought only when I had money. Later he persuaded me to take candy on credit. The debt grew beyond what I was able to repay, and so when my father gave me money to pay my school fees, I sacrificed some of it toward my debt for the candies. This was soon found out and I was reprimanded. My father then gave me more pocket money, and the school forgave him the debt I owed and even stopped charging him the token tuition.

The methods of education in the yeshiva differed little from the previous schools, but we had longer hours of study. This was to fulfill the Scripture, "but thou shalt meditate therein day and night" (Josh. 1:8); and the rabbinical dictum, "Eat bread with salt, and drink water by measure, and sleep on the hard earth, and live a life of affliction, yet keep on toiling in the study of the Torah. If thou doest thus, happy shalt thou be in this world, and it shall be well with thee in the world to come" (Abboh 6:4).

The studies were now only talmudic. The teachers recited the lecture in the *Mishna* and the *Gemara*, the two parts of the Babylonian Talmud. This also included the commentary on the Talmud by Rashi, and the *Tosaphoth*, the additional material by later rabbis meant to elucidate the text and to sharpen the mind of the student. We repeated and discussed the lecture after the teacher, and then we studied more of the Talmud by ourselves.

Thus in the yeshiva, the Talmud reigned supreme. The Old Testament Bible could be used only for reference and there were no secular studies whatsoever.

I had no contacts with Christianity at all. On the way to school we passed a Roman Catholic church and a Russian Orthodox church, and we spat, pronouncing the words found in Deuteronomy 7:26, "... thou shalt utterly detest it, and thou shalt utterly abhor it; for it is a cursed thing." I said it halfheartedly because of my previous favorable contact with Christianity and because some questions were beginning to creep into my mind. Why should we say such horrible words? The people looked so pious. They came from surrounding villages to worship, and they never bothered us.

As I continued studying the Talmud, I came to a passage that told of a cruel punishment for that Sinner of Israel, meaning Jesus. For one sin of deriding the rabbis, He was punished forever and ever with cruelty as to be "judged in boiling excrement." I did not like this story at all. Did it really mean what it said? Could I possibly be in full agreement with this? Did not I also have doubts about the rabbis' claims that their teachings were given to Moses on Mount Sinai? What then would *my* punishment be? It was many years before I dared to proclaim these doubts openly.

Life in a yeshiva in a little town in Poland becomes very dull. Day by day we had the same talmudic studies in an East Aramaic dialect spoken in Babylon fifteen hundred years ago; the same students attended year after year, except the ones who were not promoted or who dropped out. Each year we experienced the same fears—that non-Jewish boys would dislike our dress and our sidecurls, or *peyot*, and attempt to beat us up; that ghosts of dead people would appear when we had to pass near a cemetery; that the teacher would beat us up, although that rarely happened.

However, a few things happened that temporarily took me out of my depression. One was the engagement and marriage of my oldest sister, Rachel. There would have been, humanly speaking, little hope of Rachel being married, since every Jewish girl in that part of the world needed a dowry.

However, my father had inherited some of the fields that had belonged to my paternal grandfather. These were now sold, and a matchmaker was called in and told what dowry my father was able to give. The matchmaker found a husband for Rachel, a carpenter of Ruda-Huta. At the time it meant little to me except that I was glad to enjoy a few days away from school and to eat the goodies prepared for the feast. Unfortunately my father had to borrow additional money from a neighbor, a German Lutheran settler, at a high interest rate and could not repay the debt. (In later years after the German invasion into Poland, he was beaten for the unpaid debt.)

Another important event in my life at this time was my Bar Mitzva. At the age of thirteen a Jewish son becomes a "Son of the Commandment"; now he himself is responsible to fulfill God's laws and commandments.

The Jewish tradition is that up to the time of the Bar Mitzva, the child is free from the ceremonial laws and his father is responsible for his moral misdeeds. For weeks I, as a Bar Mitzva candidate, was taught how to put on the phylacteries in the right order. First, one phylactery is put on the left arm opposite the heart and then the other is put on the head between the eyes to fulfill the fourfold command of Exodus 13:9, 16; Deuteronomy 6:8 and 11:18. All of these passages state the following command in similar words:

And thou shalt bind them for a sign upon thine hand, and they shall be as frontlets between thine eyes.

The more religious Jews had two pairs of phylacteries: one pair was for general use, according to Rashi; and the other pair, according to the order of Rabbenu Tam, was put on after reciting the general prayers. With this second pair they recited the Shema. Thus they were sure they fulfilled the commandment in any case.

The sermon I was taught to deliver on my Bar Mitzva day centered around the stringent rabbinical warning against "the skull that had not put on phylacteries." I was called up to the reading of the Torah and pronounced the benedictions. My father thereupon blessed God for having released him from the punishment and responsibility of his child. We had a celebration with wine, whiskey, and cookies. Now I was a man. When a minyan was needed, I could complete the needed quorum. But I did not have much time to dwell on these thoughts, as school and studies were pressing, and I wanted to excel in learning as well as in piety.

At this time rumors were circulating that a number of students in the famous Lublin Yeshiva, which was led by the great Rabbi Meir Shapiro, were "yielding to the missionaries' persuasions." We could not comprehend it. How could a religious Jew reject the faith of his fathers and join a Gentile, pagan religion?

A few weeks later I was home for the weekend, and my father went shopping in town. When he returned before sunset on Friday, he brought home the Sabbath provisions and also a book which he obtained in town free of charge. The book in Yiddish was entitled *The Divine Personality of the God of Israel*, by

David L. Cooper. After I read a few pages in which the author attempted to point out that the Hebrew word *Elohim* for God is plural, it seemed blasphemous. I suggested to my parents that the book be put into the fire, for it taught Jewish people to believe in many gods. Had I read the book to the end, as I did later, I would have seen that the author was not advocating many gods, but the one Triune God.

I must also mention a certain Jewish man who contributed much to my religious life and education. This was Reb Yudl Wishnitzer, who provided my lodging and my food each Sabbath. He was a *radziner hasid*, a follower of the rabbi of Radzin, a town in central Poland. This rabbi distinguished himself and his followers by having blue threads in their fringes. He also was a *kabbalist*, believing that in addition to the simple interpretation of the Scriptures, there is also a mystical meaning to each letter. These interpretations were incorporated in the mystical book called *Zohar*, which also purported to reveal much about God, His nature, and His attributes.

He made a living by selling second-hand shoes to Jewish people. He paid no taxes and had no permit for peddling. Thus he lived in constant fear of the authorities. For his wares he traveled to Warsaw, and in the market place he would buy up several sacks of old shoes. When he came home, he would clean and repair them to sell to Jewish men and women who could not afford new shoes.

For a time business was good and Reb Yudl decided to bring electricity into the house. This was a great improvement upon the kerosene lamp, but the prosperity was only short-lived. New shoes became less expensive, and another Jewish man found out that this was a good way to make a living. Reb Yudl lost out. He could no longer afford the money to travel to Warsaw, and soon I had to find another Jewish home to provide my Sabbath food. Reb Yudl did not pay his rent for many months and finally the owner went to court and had the family, including me, evicted. It was fortunate that it was toward the end of the semester. Some Jewish people intervened on his behalf, and the Yudl's moved into a basement apartment for a very low rent. However, I could not stay with them any longer.

The many ups and downs of this life had quite a wearing effect on my family and me. My father consulted with my teachers about my future, and the decision was at last made to send me to Warsaw. There my maternal uncle took me in until I found the right school and accommodations. When the High Holy Days were over and I had collected the necessary recommendations, I set off for my further studies.

6

THE CHELMER FOOL

Since I had good credentials and recommendations, I had no difficulty being accepted into one of the best talmudical seminaries in Warsaw. At the seminary our food was provided in a dining hall, but the food was not the best. Pious Jewish women, *gabetes*, collected the food from Jewish merchants in the bazaars and market places. There was no charge for food or education at the seminary since the salaries and all expenses were provided by Reb Nathan Spigelglass and his father Ezekiel, who were among the richest Jews in Warsaw. In addition, Reb Nathan was also the honorary head of the yeshiva, and each month he delivered a lecture on the Talmud to the seniors. How grateful I was that now I did not have to go to different houses for my meals, and I could always be on time for classes.

In a short time I was recommended to a shoemaker who wanted a student to sleep in his store to protect his wares from theft. The pay was low, but as the days went by, a student who graduated recommended me to a store that offered me double the amount of pay for the same duties. I was given a key to the back door so I could leave to be in time for classes. All seemed well, but it did not work out as I expected.

The pride of our school was that we were studying Torah for its own sake, as the Talmud prescribes, and not even toward the purpose of being ordained a rabbi. This might well come later on, but our studies were entirely spiritual, not worldly. If one were ordained a rabbi, one could specialize, with the permission of the school, by studying the Jewish codes of law and its commentaries. This would be easier study than some parts of the Talmud; however, it involved memorizing the final decisions arrived at for the interpretation of respective laws.

The school was divided into four levels. I started with the first level, but was soon promoted to the second, where the teacher was the father of the teacher in the first level. He was inferior to his son in learning, but they could not put the son above the father.

They say in Yiddish, "The apple does not fall far from the tree," but in this case the differences between father and son were immense. I disliked the father as much as he disliked me. He began to call me "Chelmer fool," and I could not tolerate the idea that an old rabbi should lower himself to call a poor student names. (Of course, in the street it was common to call the people of our city fools. Nobody knows when the people of Chelm began to be called fools but the name stuck, and ignorant people thought that by humiliating others they were exalting themselves.)

Unfortunately the lectures did not really challenge me. I had begun the study of the Talmud before I was eight years old, and I was now approaching fifteen. After a few weeks the talmudic explanations of my discouraging teacher simply had nothing new in them for me, and my thoughts began to wander. He was quick to notice and would say, "Chelmer fool, explain the passage we are now discussing." I did this, to the giggles of the students and to his embarrassment. This only put him in a rage and left me helpless. He reviled me and went to the head of the yeshiva, who gave me an additional tongue-lashing. My only hope was that I would get promoted to the next level, where they had a more learned and gracious teacher. But my hopes were cruelly shattered. The principal informed me that because of my misbehavior I would have to stay in the same class. I was most humiliated and depressed. My thoughts wandered even more during the second go-around of these simplified lectures. This put my teacher in still a greater rage, but he did not ask me any more about the place and the subject he was discussing.

Two of my close friends among the students of the yeshiva stand out in my memory. Joshua was the closest relative of the Rabbi of Kozhenitz, who was now residing in Warsaw. He was aspiring to take the rabbi's place when the old rabbi departed into eternity. However, Joshua was not brilliant in his studies, and he came to me for help. As a reward he brought me goodies from the rabbi's house. I was also invited into the rabbi's presence for the Sabbath meal. I was given a good place at the table and offered the *shirayim*, leftovers of the rabbi, which are supposed to have great merit. My friend Joshua was already dressing like a rabbi, with long white socks to the knee over his trousers, shoes without shoelaces, a long tunic of pure silk, and sidecurls so long that he could bind them together under his chin.

My other friend was Benjamin of Sandomir. He was quite the opposite. He wore sidecurls only long enough to meet the requirements of the law. While on the street, he hid them behind his ears or put them under his hat. He dressed in long garments as was required of us, but in gray instead of black.

In outward piety I was somewhere between these two extremes, although as regards inward piety, I think I was not behind any of them.

All the pupils and teachers in our school were hassidim; that is, followers of one of the famous hassidic rabbis. Most of us did not belong to any political party, but the Jewish orthodox party *Agudah* was tolerated. My friend with the short sidelocks was suspected of belonging to the less orthodox party, *Mizrachi*. This latter party accepted the political aspirations of Zionism and participated fully in the World Zionist Movement. The Agudah, although it was in favor of the establishment of a Jewish state in Israel, did not want to belong to the Zionist organization.

My poor friend Benjamin was expelled from school because of his suspected association with the detested party. I met him in the street later, and he claimed that it had been a false accusation. He had never, in fact, belonged to the Mizrachi organization.

Someone had noticed that I was talking to him and reported me to the principal. When the new semester came, I was put on probation and could not attend the lectures, but only study in the great hall. This was too severe for me, and I dropped out of school.

I was still a long way from the kingdom of God, of course. I had been put on probation by the school to test my humility and endurance, and it was now revealed that I had little of either. I was not completely discouraged with Jewish studies, but simply fed up with the policies of that particular school. And now I was left with the task of finding a new yeshiva—one that would accomodate my growing desire for independence.

There were other yeshivas in Warsaw that provided for their students' needs in a more generous way than the one sponsored by Reb Nathan Spigelglass, and I joined one of them. It was not as famous as the former school, but what I lost in status, I gained in freedom. We had only seven or eight hours of study per day. We were even permitted to attend the meetings of the Mizrachi organization located on the same street. Most of the students did attend and I joined them. At these meetings they spoke in Hebrew with the Sephardic (Spanish) pronunciation, which I now attempted to learn; and they not only permitted but indeed encouraged the study of the *Tenach*, the Hebrew Scriptures. Since I had to spend fewer hours on Talmud study, I was able to spend time on the study of the Hebrew Bible with its commentaries.

This, in retrospect, might well have been the leading of God. I now attended to my studies of the Bible.

In the smaller yeshivas there was actually too much freedom and too little discipline. Therefore, the temptations were greater. After joining the small yeshiva on Gnoina Street, I found out about another yeshiva where the students had even more freedom and the material conditions were still better. At this school the food was provided for in another part of the city in a restaurant. So, I enrolled there and was soon brought in touch with the ordinary city people. They made me feel odd with my long black robes and head covering and the peyot and fringes. As I studied the Bible, I had less desire for talmudical studies. Only one who is familiar with both knows the world of difference between the Talmud and the Scriptures: the former, with its lengthy discussions and sophistry on a point of law; and the latter, the straightforward Word of God.

Philosophical matters passed through my mind at this time. The Jewish conceptions of salvation and eschatology are rather nebulous, yet some of the teachers thought it was their duty to teach us not only Talmud, but also a book from the Middle Ages entitled *Rod of Correction.* In this book the author tries to describe all the pains and sufferings in Gehenna for the least transgression of the Torah. In the Talmud, too, there is the story of a prominent rabbi who saved Judaism from extinction after the destruction of the temple in Jerusalem in the year A.D. 70. The Talmud says:

When Rabbi Yohanan ben Zakkai got sick, his disciples came to visit him. When he saw them, he began to cry. They said to him, Our Master, the light of Israel, the right pillar, the mighty hammer, why do you cry? He said to them, My children, you know that were they to lead me now before a king of flesh and blood—who is here today and tomorrow he may be put in the grave; if he be angry with me—his anger cannot last forever. If he kills me, he cannot kill me for eternity. Moreover, I could persuade him with my eloquence and buy him up with money—yet I would have wept. Now they are going to bring me before the king of all kings, who is alive and exists forever. If he imprisons me—his imprisonment is forever—and I cannot persuade him with eloquence or buy him up with money—not only this, but there are two ways before me—one leading into Gan-Eden, Paradise, and the other into Gehenna; and I do not know in which one they are going to lead me—should not I cry? *(Berakhot* 28:B).

If this Rabbi Yohanan was not certain, what hope was there for me? I began thinking about my near future. There was now little hope that I would get a position as a rabbi, since I had left the famous school. There were too many ordained rabbis in Poland and too much competition. I could hardly be a *shokhet*, a ritual slaughterer, for I could not watch animals being killed. There was a third possibility for me. A rich Jewish man might come looking for a son-in-law, and I might be the lucky one chosen. However, this too seemed unrealistic. Concern about the future, then, led me to my next decision.

7

THE SIGNS OF GIDEON

In the year 1936 I finally left the yeshiva for the last time. I was on my way to the friendly restaurant when I saw a friend with whom I had studied in Chelm. He was standing on a street corner selling haberdashery, and he soon persuaded me to do the same.

It was a difficult decision. Once having begun there was no way back. It would certainly have been a disgrace for the school to receive me again, since I was now merely an unconsecrated merchant. I did undertake this new career, however, and I had to look for new lodging since I was no longer in the yeshiva.

I had to find lodgings quickly, and although I did not know the Lord in a personal way, He led me to a place which ultimately led me to Him. The Jewish family with whom I found lodgings had a one-room apartment in a basement. To supplement their income they took in subtenants, about six at a time. We slept on folding cots, and the charge was a little over a dollar per month. It was better than being locked in the store, and I was happy.

Mr. Griker was a tailor, and Mrs. Griker liked to go to the "missionaries." Her husband sometimes

69

joined her, and they invited me to go with them. I refused at first, but gave in upon their insistence. Mrs. Griker told me: "My husband and I did not study the Bible much. 'They' say that Jesus is the Messiah and they show us places in their Bible to confirm it. But you who studied in the yeshiva could tell us whether they are right or wrong." This appealed to my pride, and I went with them.

The meeting took place on 53 Ogrodowa Street in Warsaw, in an inconspicuous little place on the third floor. There were about forty people there. The program started and a hymn was announced. Some joined wholeheartedly, singing in Yiddish the hymn, "I hear Thy welcome voice, that calls me Lord to Thee. ...." Others giggled. The prayer, offered by missionary Paul Rosenberg, was in Yiddish too, and this caused me to burst out laughing. I had never heard men praying in Yiddish and it seemed absurd to me. Women might do so from their own prayer books, but men would pray only in Hebrew from the authentic prayer book, the *siddur*.

I was finally reprimanded for my behavior in the service, but people must have been praying for me because my thoughts turned in a new direction. "Why must we pray in Hebrew?" I asked myself. Does God understand that language only? And how did our fathers pray in ancient times before prayer books were composed? I became quite introspective and remained so for the rest of the service.

The Bible reading and sermon were on Gideon. He is the one who asked for two signs to be sure that God truly called him, and when he was given these signs he was ready to forsake everything for God, including the religion of his family. The speaker claimed he could also show us many signs from the Word of God that Jesus is the Messiah if we were sincere and ready to face the consequences.

I suddenly shouted, "Show us, if you can!" He courteously asked me to wait until the meeting was over, and then he would.

With the Hebrew benediction, the meeting ended, and the speaker invited me to a back room. About a dozen others joined us. Mr. Rosenberg had a large Hebrew Bible in front of him and he pointed to various prophecies, which he claimed had been fulfilled in Jesus. I objected that none of these proved that it must have been that particular person. I said, "The Messiah whom the Jewish people look for will fulfill these and many other prophecies that Jesus did not fulfill."

He did not argue with me, but showed me the prophecy in Daniel 9:25–27, and began to explain how the Messiah was to be "cut off" before the city of Jerusalem and the temple were destroyed by the Romans in A.D. 70. I could not refute the point, for it was definitely written in the book that the Messiah shall "be cut off, but not for himself: and the people of the prince that shall come shall destroy the city and the sanctuary" (Dan. 9:26). Still, I was at a loss, for religious Jews hardly ever study the Scriptures only. They always consult the commentaries printed below and around the text of the Scriptures.

I admitted this frankly and told him, "Sir, we never study this book, but I will look up the references and see what our commentators have to say about it." This brought our conversation to a close. He gave me a copy of the Hebrew New Testament and expressed his conviction that I was a sincere person and that my sincerity would bring me to faith in Jesus the Messiah. Of course, I thought differently and went about my business.

Although this was certainly not the first time I had come in contact with the gospel, it was the first time I had heard it in Hebrew and Yiddish and preached by a Jewish person. Here was an intelligent Jewish man with religious and secular education, who claimed that if I were honest and sincere I would have to admit that Jesus is the Messiah.

Of course, I thought that it would be interesting to consult the rabbinical view of these verses. Perhaps I could then return and show the man how wrong he was and that he should cease leading our people astray.

The believers from the meeting were praying for me, and I became restless to such a degree that whenever I passed near a *Bet Hamidrash*, a synagogue used for prayer and study, I went inside to find the Book of Daniel with the rabbinic commentaries.

The Jewish people rarely study the Book of Daniel because many rabbinic Jews were misled attempting to interpret Daniel's cryptic "times." Some were led so far astray that they came to believe in false messiahs, and therefore talmudic Jews frowned on students who studied Daniel with a view of finding out the time of the Messiah. However, religious Jews knew that this book revealed more about Messiah than any other book.

It took quite a few weeks until I finally found the Book of Daniel with all commentaries. The commentators apparently had much difficulty with these verses, and only a few attempted to comment on this passage. All of them were following the lead of Rashi, of the eleventh century, who said the Hebrew word *mashiakh* referred to King Agrippa. Agrippa was slain shortly before the Romans destroyed the second temple.

I had hoped to return to the missionary and tell him of our superior interpretation. But somehow it was incredible, even to me, that the Messiah in Daniel should refer to King Agrippa. He was an insignificant king who ruled Israel by the permission of Rome, and he was not of the House of David. Daniel was regarded as the prophet "par excellence" of Messiah's coming. Yet, when the Hebrew word *mashiakh* was mentioned, a revelation of God after much fasting and prayer on the part of the prophet, the reference is relegated to a selfish, opulent Edomite king.

That simply could not be!

I left the House of Study perplexed. Were we wrong about Him whom the missionaries claimed to be the Messiah?

This simply could not be either, and yet how could one explain it?

I did not go back to the mission, but I turned to the Hebrew New Testament, which I had not read until now.

There is charm in the thought of a child's being brought up on the Word of God, as I was. But, of course, I had read only the Old Testament—the Hebrew Scriptures—and the purpose was to know the law, especially the ceremonial laws. As for the New Testament, I simply had no idea it existed.

Once, when my father brought home a Yiddish book distributed by the missionaries, there were some references to names and books that were not familiar to me. I did not know that these books were part of the New Testament. The thought might have occurred to me that Gentiles perhaps had their Bibles, just as we had ours. I had seen people going to church carrying small black books. I imagined that the contents must be much inferior to our Torah and that perhaps the books contained teachings about the inferiority of the Jews, just as our books tell about our election and superiority to all nations. Perhaps they also contained hate passages against us, for many of the pogroms and the Spanish Inquisition began in the church.

There was, therefore, an unusual charm and a happy surprise for me when I opened to the first verse, Matthew 1:1, and read, "This is the generation of *Yeshua Hamashiakh* [Jesus the Messiah], the Son of David, the Son of Abraham."

When my mother later began reading the New Testament, she asked me one day, "Why are the religious Jews so much against you and against this Book? I find only good things in it." It was also a pleasant "disappointment" for her, seeking only evil and finding only good and holy things in that little Book, so Jewish and yet so universal. It linked directly to the Old Testament, pointed out prophecies that were fulfilled, and told of the best Jew of all mankind who lived in the land of Israel at a crucial time in our history. He repaid good for evil, and His major concern was with the poor, the neglected, and the rejected. He healed the sick, restored sight to the blind, unstopped the ears of the deaf, and even brought life to the dead. His teaching was not only in the spirit of the prophets, but was holier, more sublime, and upheld the Scripture. How could we have been ignorant of such a Book?

As I read on in the New Testament, I knew for sure that Jesus of Nazareth was the Messiah—not just because of the prophecy of Daniel 9:25–27, but because of the many other wonderfully fulfilled prophecies in the life of this Man. I knew the Old Testament, and it was crystal clear to me that if the Hebrew Scriptures of the Old Testament were true, then the New Testament was the continuation and consummation of these Scriptures and therefore must be true also. The New Testament claimed that God fulfilled His promises and prophecies by sending Jesus as Messiah and Savior. This then must also be true.

If there was a shred of reason left in me, I had to believe that Jesus was the promised Savior and Messiah. I therefore believed and was satisfied.

It may sound simple, but that's all that happened when I came to the Messiah. There were no tears, no marching up an aisle, and no celebrations. I was simply a person well studied in God's Word in the Old Testament. I now had verified the truth of the New Testament. I knew myself to be a sinner, and I was repentant. Therefore, all that was necessary was the knowledge of who my Savior actually was. The New Testament is written expertly as a witness to Jewish people and all other peoples. It saved me.

Among Jewish believers in the Messiah today, the term "conversion" is rarely used. We speak rather of the new believer as being a "completed Jew." The term "conversion" is not well liked by the Jews; our people usually think of converting from one religion to another, or as the Yiddish expresses it, *toyshen dos rendl*, changing the coin. We vehemently deny that we have exchanged our Jewish coin for a non-Jewish coin; and therefore we prefer, from the semantic point of view, not to use that phrase.

The biblical conversion, however, has nothing to do with such a conception. The Word of God refers to the conversion of the sinner, the conversion of the heart and mind from being far away from God to full fellowship with Him, our Creator. Such a conversion is needed for Jew and Gentile alike. However, my conversion, or completion, was only from ignorance and unbelief to recognition and belief in Jesus the Messiah.

My heart was not changed as yet, and therefore I did not return to the place where I was first challenged with the gospel. Because of my pride, it was too difficult for me to acknowledge that the missionary was right and I was wrong. As I continued peddling in the streets, I was handed an invitation to meetings, which also offered English classes. There I began to attend the English classes and the Hebrew-Yiddish meetings led by Moses H. Gitlin.

My desire increased to learn more about this newly discovered Messiah and New Testament. My heart was also softened and I realized that I should return to the place where I first heard about Jesus, but the man who first proclaimed the truth to me had gone to South America. It was a great disappointment. However, one evening Miss Tordis Christoffersen, who was in charge of the mission, spoke in her usual broken Yiddish about the Tabernacle, showing how this points to Christ and His work as a sacrifice for sin.

I was deeply impressed by it. Every morning, as a

religious Jew, I proudly recited my prayers, which contain the words: "Blessed be the Lord our God, the King of the world, that He did not make me a *goy* [Gentile]," and again, "Blessed be the Lord God, King of the world, that He did not make me a woman." But here was a Gentile woman who knew more of the Jewish Bible and its spiritual meaning than I, who had spent many years studying the Torah and Talmud from early morning till late at night! My pride was completely gone, and when she called for repentance from sin and for prayer, I knelt with others and poured out my heart before God asking Him to be merciful to me, a proud, selfish sinner. This was my conversion from unforgiven sins to the acceptance of the sacrifice of the Lord Jesus on the altar of Golgotha.

The greatest work of this mission was done in the summer months. They had a summer camp in the little town of Radosc, a suburb of Warsaw. This villa and the surrounding grounds were called Bethel. Jewish children from the city were taken for two to four weeks, and they rejoiced to get out of the city. I was invited to stay at the camp for the summer as a volunteer colaborer. My work was mostly physical—repainting the outside of the villa and the fences, and watering the flower and vegetable beds. I also taught the children Bible verses in Yiddish and Hebrew. An elderly man from the United States, Mr. McGaw, gave me daily lessons in the Gospel of John.

The summer was almost over when one morning a tall policeman appeared on the grounds and asked for me. I had peddled in the streets without a permit and had not paid the fine, and now the law had caught up with me. I was sentenced to forty-eight hours imprisonment.

I was taken to what looked like a tool shed. It contained a long, large box. This was to be my chair and bed. In such arrests the prisoner was given no food unless a friend or relative brought him some, and everything was taken away lest he commit suicide. However, they apparently overlooked my Hebrew New Testament, which I had in my vest pocket.

I read it again, from beginning to end, and then reread it more slowly. When I came to the words in 2 Corinthians 4:16, I had to stop and meditate on them. "For which cause we faint not; but though our outward man perish, yet the inward man is renewed day by day." I realized that the apostle Paul must have had a personal relationship with his Messiah, such as I had never experienced. Would this be available also for me? My outward conditions did not matter now. All that mattered was the inward man and the Messiah. I prayed and God answered my prayers. My spirit was quickened and renewed within me. When I read along in the New Testament, there came upon me a new realization of the veil that had been before my eyes, but that now was stripped away. I was a new creation in Christ Jesus: ". . . old things are passed away; behold, all things are become new" (2 Cor. 5:17).

When released I returned to the villa Bethel and people said, "You have changed." Others asked, "Have you seen a vision?" I kept silent, for it was difficult to explain what had really happened. Now I knew for certain that the Lord Jesus was my personal Savior, Lord, and King. Things took on a new significance, as the author of the song expressed it:

> Heaven above is softer blue,
> Earth around is sweeter green;
> Something lives in every hue,
> Christless eyes have never seen.[1]

My work was no longer a chore but a joy. Complaints were gone and all was fresh and good such as I had never known before. However, summer soon ended, and we had to return to the city. Would my faith hold while I peddled my wares in the city streets? It did indeed!

Often I am asked: "What have you found in Jesus that you did not find in Judaism?"

In answer, I want to state my great admiration and gratitude to my own people. One can hardly improve on the apostle Paul, who described his indebtedness to this people in the following words:

> I say the truth in Christ, I lie not, my conscience also bearing me witness in the Holy Ghost, That I have great heaviness and continual sorrow in my heart. For I could wish that myself were accursed from Christ for my brethren, my kinsmen according to the flesh: Who are Israelites; to whom pertaineth the adoption, and the glory, and the covenants, and the giving of the law, and the service of God, and the promises; Whose are the fathers, and of whom, as concerning the flesh Christ came, who is over all, God blessed for ever (Rom. 9:1–5).

---

[1]From the hymn "I Am His and He Is Mine."

To paraphrase those thoughts, we could say that all of Christianity and the whole world is indebted to the Jewish people for their three major contributions:

1. Monotheism. Egypt had its triune god-system with Osiris, Iris, and Horus as the chief group, and in addition the sun god to whom the city of Heliopolis was dedicated. Greece was reveling in relating the achievements, the tricks, the seditions, the adulteries, and even the impotence of their gods in face of one another and in face of *moira*, the unexplained and fearsome fate. Mighty Rome was worshiping Jove, Venus, Mars, Mercury, and Bacchus. Israel alone proclaimed: "Hear, O Israel, the Lord our God, the Lord is One."

2. The Bible. "Unto them were committed the oracles of God" (Rom. 3:2).

3. The Lord Jesus. "Of whom as concerning the flesh Christ came" (Rom. 9:5).

I also know that when the Gentile world hates me, I will find solace and comfort among my people, whom I can always trust.

Yet, notwithstanding those things listed above, Judaism will always remain incomplete without Messiah Jesus. To me it is clear that:

1. Judaism without Jesus is promise without

fulfillment. What is the value of the prophecy "The Redeemer coming to Zion," when He never came; "Unto Him shall the gathering of the people be" (Gen. 49:10) when there was never a Jew to whom the people, the nations, gathered?

2. Prophecy would be idealistic not realistic. Isaiah says: "I will also give thee for a light to the nations, that thou mayest be my salvation unto the end of the earth" (Isa. 49:6). The Lord Jesus is the only realization of such prophecy.

3. Without Jesus, our God would be called a universal God who ignores three and a half billion people and has provided salvation for one half of one per cent of the world's population, the Jews.

4. Without Jesus there is no provision of dealing with sin, for the two thousand years since the temple destruction. There is no provision for sacrifice, as required by Jewish law.

5. Judaism without Jesus cannot explain adequately Isaiah 53, "By His stripes we are healed," and a host of similar Scriptures about the sacrificial mission of the Messiah.

8

FRYDLAND, THE GOY?

There were four Jewish mission stations in Warsaw. The oldest was the Anglican mission led by Rev. Martin Parsons and Rev. Jacob Jocz. They had their main meetings on Sundays. Another mission on Ogrodowa Street was associated with the Mildmay Mission to the Jews. There were also two American Jewish missions: the one where I first heard the gospel, which had its meetings on Friday evenings, and the one sponsored by the American Board of Missions to the Jews, with meetings Saturday afternoons. As a new believer, I was hungry for the Word of God, and I attended *all* the meetings. Then the mission on Ogrodowa Street introduced free English classes taught by Miss Grace Collidge, and, having free time, I began to attend the classes.

When I came for the third lesson, Mr. Sendyk, who was in charge of the mission, called me in for a private talk. He told me that since he had been in charge, he had lost his young coworker, Mr. Troper, who had died from blood poisoning, and he wanted me to take his place. This was a great surprise to me. I drew his attention to the newness of my faith and my inexperience, and also that I had not even been baptized. However, he still offered me the position, and my appointment began in November, 1937. On January 15, 1938, Pastor Gitlin baptized me in the Polish Baptist Church of Warsaw, although I was to join the German Baptist Church to which Mr. Sendyk belonged.

The work was not new to me. Since the day when I began to believe in the Lord Jesus, I was compelled to witness to my friends and relatives, to the people who came to the mission, and to all who knew me and wanted to know the reason for the change that had taken place within me. As I attended the mission meetings and discussions developed, the questions were often addressed to me. The Lord had enabled me to explain the hope that was within me. Now there was a full opportunity to serve the Lord and the chance to leave my street peddling. I had given up peddling anyway, since it was illegal and therefore unfit for a believer in the Messiah. I could see the hand of the Lord leading and guiding, not only since I believed, but even before that. The Word of God says, "While we were yet sinners, Christ died for us" (Rom. 5:8).

When I was in the yeshiva, I rarely wrote home, but now I became more convinced that I must tell my parents what had happened. Yet whenever I began to write about my faith, I lacked the courage to be frank and I wrote in an indirect way. They must have guessed, or perhaps others wrote and told them of my experience because on a certain day, unannounced, my mother came to visit me.

After so many years of separation, she burst out in tears—tears that should have been of joy to see me. However, now they were tears of sorrow because of the humiliations she had undergone from some

Jewish people who blamed her and my father for my "departure from Judaism." In their deep suffering they went to the hassidic rabbi who advised them to talk with me.

What can one say to a mother who points to the deep wounds inflicted on her by others because of one's behavior? I kept silent for I knew the pain in her heart, but I told her that it was done, it could not be changed, it was a personal matter, and that I had not become a *goy*.

We went to have our meals in a kosher Jewish restaurant. My behavior and speech were Jewish as before, and I treated her better than I ever had before. She went home comforted.

A few weeks later my father came and stayed with me. People had told him that when a Jewish person is baptized, a cross is branded on his left arm in the place where he used to put on the phylacteries. My father checked that carefully and saw that there was no branded cross on my arm. He reasoned that if I had become a *goy*, I should have been given a Gentile name. He looked in my documents and my name was still the same.

What then had happened? I explained to him as best I could. In the evening we had a meeting at the mission. My father listened quietly. The next day we went to see Rev. Gitlin, my teacher, and my father found nothing wrong there either. We spent the rest of our time together with several of my sisters in Warsaw.

My father also went home comforted. He was now sure that his only son had not become a *goy* and had not joined the enemies of the Jews to help them persecute his people. He felt that the Jewish fanatics must be wrong, for his son was not branded with a cross as they had told him, but continued to speak Yiddish and to keep his Jewish name.

The world situation was becoming dark. Hitler had become ruler of Germany in 1933, but those around me seemed unconcerned. The Jewish people in Poland had their own troubles. We read of the foreign problems in the newspapers, but went about our own business. However, an exodus of German Jews started because those who were born outside Germany were compelled to return to their own countries. Thousands of refugees began to swell the Jewish community of Warsaw. All day they searched for work in the city. In the evening they needed places where they would be welcome. At the mission they found an open door, and if they were hungry they would also find some relief. They were not opposed to faith in Messiah, but wanted to understand it and to have it explained. We had a full house every night.

One evening a poor, elderly Jewish refugee came, and I shared some food and tea with him. However, he became weak and could not move, so I called a *droshka* (a horse-driven carriage), carried him outside, paid his fare, and sent him home. Someone reported this to a Jewish paper and on the following day there was an article of a Jewish *galakh*,[1] with my name given, who helped poor refugees to win them away from Judaism.

This merely helped the cause of the gospel, for others now came to find out the truth of what they

[1]Galakh: derogatory name for a Christian, especially Roman Catholic, clergyman.

had read in the newspaper. We were most happy with a small group of five young Jewish men who began to attend the meetings. They wanted to know more of the basis of our faith and asked me to teach them systematically the Old Testament prophecies relating to the Messiah. In due time all of the group except one asked to be baptized after they received the Lord Jesus as Messiah and personal Savior. As far as I know, only one of these faithful ones survived the war. The others I could not trace.

It was a good life: In the morning I studied; in the afternoon I did house-to-house visitation and tract distribution; and in the evening there were the meetings at the mission, followed by instruction to these young men. Two nights a week I also attended public school for adults. The schedule was heavy and demanding, but I was young and able to do the work satisfactorily.

9

SEPTEMBER 1, 1939

Oh that my head were waters,
and mine eyes a fountain of tears,
that I might weep day and night
for the slain of the daughter of my people!
—Jeremiah 9:1

September 1, 1939, in Warsaw, Poland, did not seem to be different from any other day. The autumn weather was pleasant and the air was fresh and crisp. I had experienced blessings in recent days of being alone with the Lord and was encouraged by the fellowship with young believers—seeing them grow in the Lord—and my heart was filled with joy to overflowing.

But the sirens were sounded and people began to take shelter. Others, as I did, thought it was just another air-raid test and kept on about their business. I was on my way to the Jewish district on Nalewki Street near the Krasinski Park and had proceeded less than half a block on my way when the bombs began to fall nearby. So I too took shelter within one of the gates of the Warsaw tenement houses. The alarm was called off for awhile and I returned to our mission on Ogrodowa Street.

We soon knew that the war was a reality. Mr. Sendyk, in charge of the mission, had a radio and we heard the grim news. The other young men came in, and we considered our situation. If we left Warsaw, where would we go?

We went to the market and bought some provisions, but there was little left to buy.

The bombing increased daily. Before dawn we were out to stand in line for bread at the bakery, but only once were we fortunate enough to bring home a loaf. Our meager provisions were soon gone. The electricity supply was bombed, as well as the gas and water supplies. When the bombings lessened, we ran quickly through the streets to find a slain horse so that we could cut a piece of it for food. We risked our lives to carry home a bucket of water from the Vistula River, which flows through Warsaw, or a few pieces of wood from bombed-out houses.

Tension in the city was high. The Polish population was humiliated, and they were seeking a scapegoat. The people in our tenement house noticed us, and said, "Such young, strong men, and you are cowering here instead of joining the volunteers for the defense of our city." We were afraid of these angry people and we knew we should volunteer. There was no food to be had and anyway we were in constant danger, day and night, from the bombs. Three of us, at the ages of nineteen and twenty, went for induction. We were given uniforms and rifles, and a Protestant clergyman led us in the oath of induction.

We were given certificates showing that we now

belonged to the Volunteer Batallion for the Defense of Warsaw. The training was a sham. An officer came for a few minutes and showed us how to use a rifle and how to throw a grenade so that it did not explode in our hands. We had to take shelter every few minutes, for the Germans knew every move we made.

I told the officer of my convictions and that I would prefer serving in a capacity that did not involve killing people. He agreed that my duties would be to take care of two horses and a wagon, and to travel with them under fire. I would supply the soldiers at the front and rescue whatever possible from the burning supply stores. It was a miracle that I was not seriously hurt, and that the horses were able to avoid the pot holes in the streets of Warsaw, as well as to survive the bombing that went on constantly. The words of Psalm 91 became a reality as never before.

He that dwelleth in the secret place of the most High shall abide under the shadow of the Almighty.

I will say of the Lord, He is my refuge and my fortress: my God; in him will I trust.

Surely he shall deliver thee from the snare of the fowler, and from the noisome pestilence.

He shall cover thee with his feathers, and under his wings shalt thou trust: his truth shall be thy shield and buckler.

Thou shalt not be afraid for the terror by night; nor for the arrow that flieth by day;

Nor for the pestilence that walketh in darkness; nor for the destruction that wasteth at noonday.

A thousand shall fall at thy side, and ten thousand at thy right hand; but it shall not come nigh thee.

Only with thine eyes shalt thou behold and see the reward of the wicked.

Because thou hast made the Lord, which is my refuge, even the most High, thy habitation;

There shall no evil befall thee, neither shall any plague come nigh thy dwelling.

For he shall give his angels charge over thee, to keep thee in all thy ways.

They shall bear thee up in their hands, lest thou dash thy foot against a stone.

Thou shalt tread upon the lion and adder: the young lion and the dragon shalt thou trample under feet.

Because he hath set his love upon me, therefore will I deliver him: I will set him on high, because he hath known my name.

He shall call upon me, and I will answer him: I will be with him in trouble; I will deliver him, and honor him.

With long life will I satisfy him, and shew him my salvation (Ps. 91:1–16).

One sad day the shooting stopped and it became known that Warsaw had surrendered. The military officials gave us a few cans of food, a little money, some civilian clothing, and we returned to our homes. One of our group was slightly wounded, but Jonah Kukawka and I came home safe and sound. In a few days, the man who was wounded recovered and came back also, for the Germans released all Jewish soldiers taken captive.

They considered Jews unworthy to be prisoners of war.

Later we found out to our sorrow that in their perfidy they released the Jewish prisoners so that when the time came to kill the Jews, they would not transgress the Geneva Convention, which forbids the killing of prisoners of war. But for the time being at least, we were happy to be home.

There was little to do in the city. The few belongings I had left in the mission had been sold, for they thought I had perished while in the army. Perhaps hunger compelled them to sell my possessions. Our pastor, Mr. Fester, had moved into the mission apartment because his house was bombed out. I talked over my problems with him and asked him to give me a certificate of baptism, which perhaps would be helpful to me. Having this, I decided to leave the starving city and make my way back to the farm where I could work and earn my living.

About seventy miles north of Warsaw, as one follows the Vistula, is the ancient city of Plock, with many evangelical villages surrounding it. I had been there for my vacations, helping with the farmwork, and now that I had additional experience in the army with horses and wagon, I thought it would be a good place to earn my living.

I slung my knapsack with my few possessions on my shoulders and headed north, hoping to find physical and spiritual food. It took hours to cross the burning city of Warsaw. As I was leaving, German troops were marching into the fallen city, singing their songs of victory.

As noon approached, I was hungry and I was not yet even out of the city. I was desperate for food. Finally I came upon an abandoned field, and like many others I dug out a few potatoes. I hoped that perhaps later I would find a place to make a fire and bake them in the ashes.

I was full of these dreams of filling my stomach when I was stopped by one of the S.S. soldiers, who later became our tragically familiar enemies.

"Halt!" he shouted.

I stopped, of course.

"Bist du Jude?"[1]

It was the first time I was addressed in such a way. It had not occurred to me that being Jewish might be a crime! But I had an evil foreboding from the experiences I had heard about. When the German army entered Warsaw, a friend told me they distributed hot soup to the starving population. A Hebrew Christian friend of mine stood in line with many others. When his turn finally came, the soldier who doled out the soup recognized him to be a Jew, and instead of soup he received a beating. He returned to the mission hungry and humiliated.

Thus, when the S.S. soldier shouted, instead of answering, I showed him my certificate from the German Baptist Church. He spat at me, *"Ja, aber du bist doch Jude."*[2] He grabbed a shovel and hit me over the back with such force that I fell down into a ditch where a few other Jews were burying dead horses.

Humiliated, I began to weep. The other Jewish people tried to comfort me. It was not that I was concerned for the beating, but for the fact that I belonged to a church that was identified with the German people. In this church I had learned to appreciate the Protestant Christianity that came to us in Poland via the German people; that these very

[1] "Are you a Jew?"
[2] "Yes, but you are a Jew for all that."

people should behave in such a cruel way was too much for me at this moment.

I began working with these Jewish people. As evening approached, we were taken to an unfinished building, without roof, windows, doors, or floors. Some of us had matches and we made a fire, putting our potatoes into the ashes. We ate them half raw, since hunger was pressing upon us. I began to pray quietly, wondering what would happen to us. Somehow I felt led to leave. The others protested, saying, "They will kill you." But none of the soldiers noticed me. I did not return to the highway but decided I would make my way north via the forest.

Suddenly a soldier stood in front of me. "What are you doing here? Don't you know there is a death penalty for walking in the forests where there are still abandoned guns and military equipment?"

This time I did not answer, but just made motions to my mouth that I was hungry and looking for food.

Then he said quietly, "I am a Czech and I sympathize with you," and he gave me half a loaf of bread. It was green inside from staleness, but who could describe the feeling of eating bread after three weeks of being without!

After further warning by the soldier, I returned to the highway. It was dusk and I wanted to stay overnight in the home of a peasant. The Polish peasants had always been hospitable, but I discovered that a law now existed that no Aryan was permitted to have a non-Ayran, a Jew, spend the night in his house. One friendly peasant said, "There is a heap of soft straw outside, and you can sleep there; but as it were, without my knowledge."

I arose early in the morning to continue my walk

north. Within a few miles there was a store where food was plentiful at almost prewar prices. I ate as much as I needed and was strengthened. In some towns there remained Jews and they received me gladly, with no questions. I continued on my way until I finally reached my destination. The Christian believers took me in and brought me back to health.

I wrote to the Jewish believers in Warsaw that there was abundance of provisions here, and one of the Jewish believers came to join me. However, our joy was short-lived, as this district was incorporated into the German Reich (Empire). Our Christian friends were warned not to keep us, and soon I was forced to leave. The decree came out that Jews in the Reich territory were to wear yellow patches on the front and back of their clothing. If I wore them, I could not stay in a non-Jewish home. If I did not wear them, there was the death penalty to face.

Slowly I began my trip back to Warsaw. Now I was more experienced as to which roads to avoid and what hours to walk. After four days I arrived in Warsaw. It would have been faster by bus or boat, but Jews were not permitted to use any public transportation—bus, boat, or train.

On my first day back I found out that my sister Esther had died of typhus, and Rebecca had also been sick with the disease. I went to see her and found her head shaved because of the sickness. Her husband was missing, and she did not know what had happened to him. My youngest sister, Judith, was alive and well. Also my oldest sister, Rachel, and her family in Lodz were alive. The food situation in the city had improved, but only for those who had sacks of money. Everything cost at least a hundred times more than it had before the war. Meat and other luxuries increased two hundredfold in price. Many of my friends existed by selling their clothing and other household items to the peasants for food. The money I had would not be enough to buy food even for two days.

As I passed by the streets in the Jewish district, I noticed walls being erected with the inscriptions on the top, *SEUCHENGEFAHR,* "Danger of typhus. Keep away." I was informed, however, that the real purpose of the walls was to enclose the Jews in a special ghetto.

I bade farewell to my sisters and friends, bought some pins and laces wholesale, which I could exchange for food, and I set out walking the 120 miles to the village where my parents lived. Before I left, I had prayer and fellowship with the leading Hebrew Christians of Warsaw, all half-starved, yet maintaining their faith and witness.

It was already the middle of December when I reached the town of Chelm, only four miles away from our village of Lesniczowka. I entered the home of our relatives on 26 Oblonska Street, and they stared at me as if I were a ghost. When they comprehended that I had actually passed through the streets of Chelm, they told me what had happened there. That morning all Jewish males were ordered to report to the market place to hear a speech. Some were afraid and hid themselves, as did one of the men in this house. The majority that went were dragged to the river Bug. Most of them were killed on the way because they could not go as fast as the S.S. soldiers who accompanied them. The ones that reached the destination were driven into the partially frozen river, which was the new frontier between Germany and Russia.

The Russians on the other bank did not understand what was happening and began shooting. The Germans returned fire from their side, and the Jewish men in the water provided target practice. Only a few survived this death march.

I had some refreshments and hastened home to my parents. They could hardly believe I was truly alive. I told them that Esther had died and they began the seven days of mourning, called *shiv'a*.

The articles I brought home were sold to the peasants for food, and this helped. Soon I began to work on the farms, and so we had an adequate food supply. My sister Rebecca also came home from Warsaw and found work easily as a tailoress among the peasants, and they gave her food in payment for her work. By God's grace, we lived satisfactorily and hoped that the Allies would soon defeat the Nazis and that we would be able to resume normal living.

The years from 1939 to 1942 were years of great danger and utmost restrictions. We were ordered to hand over all metal items, which Germany needed for her war efforts against the Allies. Fortunately we did not have much of this world's riches. My mother had brass candleholders which she used for the Sabbath candles. They were her parents' wedding gift to her. We delivered them under the threat of the death penalty, along with my father's hanukah brass lamp.

Also, it was made a law that every Jew and Jewess, children and adults, had to wear an armband on the left arm. This was a special "privilege" granted to the Jews in the General Government—territories which were not incorporated into the German Reich. Apparently Jewish leaders had given much money to achieve this concession for us, as otherwise we would have been compelled to wear the yellow patches with the word *JUDE* in front and back. This would have been more humiliating.

The third oppressive law was that of the ghetto. Cities having a large Jewish population had to have Jewish ghettos, limited areas surrounded by walls and barbed wire. The Jews had to remain within the walls or face death if they climbed over them. But the city of Chelm had hardly any menfolk left because of the death marches, and thus the Jews in this city had this special privilege of not having a walled-in ghetto. There was, however, a death penalty for any Jew who left the city or his village.

This meant I could not go into the city very often, and yet it was important that I go there. I needed the Christian fellowship at the small Baptist church. My parents needed the Jewish religious items, like candles for Friday night to welcome the Sabbath, or a chicken slaughtered by a Jewish shokhet, so that it would be kosher. Otherwise they could have no authentic Sabbath. So from time to time I risked my life and went to town for their needs and also to have fellowship with other Christians.

I was in a most peculiar situation, living with Jews, my own family, and believing in Christ. I needed the love of my family and the fellowship of the believers in the Messiah. Surrounded by enemies, I continued my pilgrimages and began to feel that the end of my life was drawing near.

10

THE LORDLY PEOPLE

Everyone knew about the cruelties perpetrated by these Nazis who called themselves *Herrenvolk*, the lordly people. The people in the asylums for the mentally ill were the first ones to succumb to these cruelties. They were herded together and shot with dum-dum bullets, which blew their brains out. Then came the cruelties of the death marches for the male population. The ones that survived were then commanded to live in ghettos surrounded by walls. In the few towns where Jews were permitted to remain without a ghetto wall, they were nevertheless forbidden to leave their town and always had to wear the armband with the star of David. Whenever a German soldier approached, Jews had to get off the sidewalk and take off their hats while the soldier passed by. Otherwise they would be beaten, often to the point of death.

One Friday I went to town to have the chicken ritually slaughtered so that my parents could eat meat that week. A soldier was coming toward me. By law I should have stepped down from the sidewalk and taken off my hat, but being nearsighted, I did not notice him. He hit me over my head with a blow that broke my glasses and all was "stars" in front of me. Had he asked for my documents, which would have proved that I was not from the city in which he found me, I would have been killed.

For most of the remainder of the war I went without a hat and had no glasses.

Then our German neighbor, Otto Hubscher, joined the elite corps of the S.S. I was on my way to town one day, and some people warned me not to return home. Hubscher was lurking nearby, but I continued on my way, thinking that since he was our neighbor and knew me as a Christian, he would not harm me. However, he was drunk and he stopped me. He pointed his gun at me and began to chide and beat me, saying, "You Jews cheat us constantly." The blood began to flow from a wound on my head and all my pleading was in vain. I could do nothing more than run. But he, being drunk, could not get his gun to work; neither could he chase me. I had to slow my pace because the bleeding did not stop. The mile that separated me from the city now took hours and I arrived just before curfew. Friends insisted that I go to see a doctor immediately.

The doctor gave little hope that I would survive, for the wound had accumulated dirt and dust on the way, but he cleansed it and put on bandages. The wound began to heal but complications developed. I could eat nothing and was vomiting blood continually. However, prayer and medicine helped, and two weeks later I felt better. My mother risked her life and came to see me. She told me they had also beaten my father, but he had not suffered as much as I had and now felt better. In a few days I was able to go home and be with my parents again.

A few months later the time came for me to go to a slave labor camp. It was early in 1941 as Germany prepared for her attack on Soviet Russia. The Germans decided to build a road between Chelm and Dorohusk on the Russo-German border and decreed that a certain number of Jews and Poles must be assigned by local governments to do the work. I was asked by the *Judenrat,* the Jewish Council, to go on its behalf, together with a few others from our district.

It was not too bad at first, as the camp was open and we could go out into the nearby villages after work. The peasants sold us bread, and later, when they refused to sell us bread, they sold a few potatoes to us that they were feeding the pigs. After a few weeks they refused to sell us even the potatoes, as pigs became high priced, and it did not pay to sell the potatoes to humans, particularly Jewish humans.

In another week or two we were not permitted to leave the compound except for work. The camp was surrounded by a fence and carefully guarded. The food lessened and we began to starve, and some died. I ran away one day but was soon caught, beaten cruelly, and taken back to work. However, since it was in any case a process of starvation, the desire for food, physical and spiritual, grew in me. I prayed and decided to run away again. One Sunday morning I dressed, climbed the fence, and went to a railway station where other peasants were waiting for the train to the city where they attended church. The Lord was surely with me, and I arrived in Ruda-Huta just in time for the Sunday morning Communion service. I told the members in the church that the Nazis would probably come for me and this might be my last time with them. However, I made it home safely. The war between Russia and Germany broke out in a few weeks, and no one bothered to hunt for me.

My visits to town were now made only on rare occasions. If my mother did not have candles for Sabbath, she hollowed two potatoes, putting in some oil and a wick and this served for the Sabbath candles. We easily did without meat, even on the Sabbath. I found two evangelical Christian families near our village with whom I could have fellowship on Sunday. They had large families and meetings took place alternately in their homes. I would stay for dinner and the evening service. They loved the Word of God and taught it in their homes.

However, this lasted only for a short time, for since they were German-speaking people, they were moved away from the General Government territories to the annexed territories that had been incorporated into the German Reich. The Polish population from these territories was resettled in the General Government.

Now the only evangelical Christians of non-German descent were in town where I, being Jewish, was not permitted to go. But the deep desire for fellowship and communion, in addition to the needs of my parents, caused me to go to town again. I was halfway to town early one Sunday morning when I saw a German soldier walking toward me. I would have deserved death on two counts: for leaving the village and for not wearing the Jewish armband. I prayed hard, not so much for life, but at least to have fellowship with those believers I had not seen for a long time, and I rededicated my life to the Lord. God answered my prayer, and when we met, the soldier passed me by.

I had become used to quick prayers and quick answers.

During my stay at home there were many opportunities for some spiritual activity and achievement. Shortly after returning to my home town, I had visited my relatives. When they had finished telling me of the horrors they had passed through, they asked me about my apostasy. "Haven't you become a goy?" I showed them my document, and they saw that I had not even changed my Jewish name. This gave me the opportunity to tell them what the Lord had done for my soul.

At home my mother said, "You can stay with us. We cannot change you, but at least do not try to change other Jewish people to become like you have." However, this promise I could not make. Our home was on a highway between the large Jewish community of Ruda-Huta and that of the town of Chelm. In the years 1940 and 1941, a constant, daily movement of Jewish people stopped in our home. They had to make a living, and so they carried the produce of the farms into town and brought back with them things which the peasants would buy. They always came before dawn, while the German sentries were still asleep. They recited a hurried prayer, rested awhile, ate some breakfast and were on their way to reach town before the sentries were awake.

In due time some of them were caught, beaten up, and their wares confiscated. However, they were not deterred until a few were killed for leaving their residences, and so the peddling stopped. Some of them spoke respectfully of my faith, but others needled me. "So let it be your Messiah, but when is He coming to save us?" My reply was that first we have to believe in Him; then, no matter what may happen to us, we will be safe in Him.

Both the silent and the spoken testimonies had their effect. First, my sister told me that she was reading my Christian literature and the New Testament and listening to conversations and discussions of Christianity. She eventually came to believe in the Lord Jesus. She would have liked to have been baptized, but preferred to wait until the war ended and there were peaceful times again. She did not survive but, praise God, was saved eternally through faith in Jesus the Messiah.

I well remember one Friday when I had been to town to satisfy the religious necessities of my parents. My mother told me how she had watched me. She saw the difference in my personality, and that I was willing to jeopardize my life for them. She was also reading the New Testament in Yiddish and said that she found only good things in this Book.

This was so new to me. There was a great change in her attitude. Previously when I came home she just tolerated my faith. Now she was herself moving toward faith in Christ. She must have talked it over with my father, for he too became kind to me. He did not hide my Bibles anymore and admitted that he himself was interested and did not find anything wrong in my Christian literature.

Here I must mention also Yocheved, the daughter of Reb Gershon, the famous children's teacher in

Ruda-Huta who had no place for me when I began attending Jewish school. When I talked with Yocheved about faith in Jesus the Messiah, she showed much interest. Since it was impossible for her to visit me so that she could learn more about Jesus, she bade me to visit her. In her home I met her father and stepmother; her own mother had died years earlier. Yocheved disclosed to me the reason for her interest in Christ. She herself was exposed to Christian influence since she had some Catholic friends. Although she was attracted to the Messiah, she hesitated, thinking that she would cease to be a member of her own people. But since she had met me, she desired to understand Christianity from a Jewish viewpoint. As we sat and talked, she wanted to offer me a piece of bread, but her stepmother became angry with her, saying that they didn't have bread to spare and must keep it for an emergency. Tears began to run down Yocheved's cheeks, and I realized what hunger can do to human beings. My thoughts then turned with gratitude to God, for although my own family had to endure the same persecutions, we had plenty of bread. (The peasants paid my sister and me with food, especially with flour. We did not have a set price for our labors, and when there was not much work, we often worked from dawn until sunset for a mere pound of flour or a piece of bread. But when the harvest-time came, I could choose the peasants who paid us more.)

The contrast was too much. Here was a new believer starving for a piece of bread, while we had sufficient in our home. I invited Yocheved to our home, and despite the dangers of her leaving the village, she came; we had many lessons about the

Messiah, God, the holy Trinity, and the fulfilled prophecies. She wanted to be baptized, and we arranged for a Polish peasant family to take us to town so that she could meet the brethren in the church and let them decide what was to be done. A Christian family in Chelm took her into their home and taught her more about the Lord Jesus, and in a few weeks she was baptized. She did not dare to return to her religious father and her angry stepmother. We talked it over in the church. From all signs there would be only a few weeks left for us to live before our turn would come to die in the extermination camps. They were already continually taking trainloads to Sobibor, the extermination place only a few miles from our home.

I liked Yocheved very much. I knew that if we could get married, we would have true fellowship together and that I could provide enough bread for both of us. Our pastor, Mr. Barchuk, was willing to take the risk and give us the blessing. Thus one night after midnight with only a few people present, and after promising that we would not name the pastor who dared to marry two Jewish people in a Christian church, the ceremony was performed. After the wedding, we went to different places so that we would not throw suspicion on anyone. Yocheved joined me in my parents' home after a few days, but she could stay only a short while. She was taken from her district to do slave labor on a nearby farm that the S.S. had taken over, and so we began our marriage in separation.

11

THE FINAL SOLUTION

In the light of what was soon to happen, these years during the war were comparatively quiet. Of course, there were incidents of cruelty by individual Nazis. The restrictions were most oppressive, and a number of people were killed for not abiding by these regulations. There was hunger and starvation, but most of the Jewish people were still living in the hope that the next Allied victory would make proud Germany ask for peace, as had happened in World War I.

Sometimes the Polish police, in the service of the Nazis, harassed us, waking us at midnight and chasing us out into the cold just to annoy us. Another time soldiers came to take away the wood from the forest. We still had a few chickens left, and they commanded us to catch them. I had to slaughter them and my mother prepared them. Then the soldiers threatened us and went away laughing. We did not mind, as we knew the tide would turn, and then we would again raise chickens and have meat.

But then the trains loaded with Jewish people began to roll by. At first they were the Jews from Czechoslovakia, who were told they were being taken to Poland to work and establish a Jewish colony. Only when they were told to undress and enter the sealed gas chambers did they realize how cruelly they had been deceived and cheated. Later the trains loaded with the Jews from the surrounding cities rolled by. These people knew well what was going to happen and some of them jumped off the train and were machine-gunned. Others escaped the bullets and came to our village to seek shelter.

We took in as many as we could, but they knew that our turn also would come, and therefore they sought shelter with the Polish peasants. However, in our district we did not have the many noble souls that made Scandinavia and Holland famous, where there were many Christians who risked their lives by taking in persecuted Jewish people. Some of our peasants told these Jews to seek shelter elsewhere as they did not want to risk their lives for their sakes. Other peasants slyly offered them hospitality, then at night robbed them, assaulted the women, and delivered them to the Nazis to be killed (for which they got a reward).

A few days before our turn came, my wife Yocheved escaped from the slave labor farm and came to join us. She had heard there that all Jews were going to be killed, and so she took a chance as she wanted us to be together when we died.

In the morning I went to work as usual. I had worked only a few hours when the son of the *Soltys*, the head of the village, came and asked for me. He told me he had to deliver me to the police. However, he gave me permission to say farewell to my parents. I found them in tears. We read the Scriptures and prayed that God would show us whether to go freely for extermination or to escape and hide as others attempted to do.

At one time as we prayed it seemed God was showing the Scripture in Isaiah 26:20, "Come, my people, enter thou into thy chambers, and shut the doors about thee: *hide thyself as it were for a little moment*, until the indignation be overpast." So we agreed that when we had the opportunity, we would run away from our captors. So as the young man led me off to the police, I asked permission to enter the home of a peasant who owed me food. When I entered the house the peasant said, "They are going to kill you. You had better run away," and so I did.

My wife soon joined me. The people in the village directed her to me. She told me that later, after I had escaped, the police came for my parents and the rest of the Jewish families and took them away to the extermination camp of Sobibor. My father, being weak and not able to walk such a long distance, was killed on the way. My sister was hiding with one of the peasants for whom she had done much work without pay, hoping they would shelter her from the police. Their house was adjacent to the forest and it was an ideal place for refuge, as one could see the police coming and escape into the trees before they reached the house.

We were soon joined by two Jewish ladies, one about twenty and the other about fifty years old. They had jumped from the train that was taking them to Sobibor and somehow they came away safely. In the village they met some good peasants who, although they did not want to give them shelter, at least directed them to us. A few days later we were joined by three young Jewish boys. Their parents were the owners of the flour mill. When the Nazis came, they confiscated the mill, and the parents escaped beyond the border to Russia. The children were left with an older sister. When the mill was first taken over, the new German owners permitted the older son to operate it. Later, when they wanted to take him away to be killed, he escaped with his two younger brothers and joined us, hoping to elude death.

We built a little hut from sticks and hay. We dug a hole to get water and went out at night into the village to beg or buy food from the peasants who owed it to us for our labors during harvest. In our free time we read the Bible together, the only book we had. We prayed that God would give us grace to endure these tribulations, and that if it was His will, we might survive the war.

Who can understand all of God's ways? He knows the end from the beginning, though we do not. One day we noticed Polish police approaching, and we ran away and hid. However, they apparently found one of our group. Either the police caught her, or she voluntarily went because she could no longer endure that kind of life. During the night the snow fell, and we knew that our fate was sealed as our footprints would give us away. The three boys left us. My sister in the village was caught and killed. The Polish family for whom she had done so much in order that they might grant her shelter in time of need showed their treachery. While the police were in the village looking for hidden Jews, Mr. Kozak, in whose house she was hiding, went and told the police to come for her. When the police took her away, they forced her to show them where we were hiding in the forest.

They found us easily as we went to the village in search for food. It was an ambush. We suddenly stood face to face with them on the border of the forest, and the shooting and chasing began.

Perhaps we again made a mistake, but we had long ago decided we should try to escape, since we were afraid they might torture us to find out who gave us food. There were large posters on the street corners proclaiming that anyone who gave a Jew food, drink, or shelter would be killed along with his family. Anyone who knew the whereabouts of a Jew and did not report him to the authorities would be sent to a concentration camp for an unlimited time. We therefore had decided always to try to escape. However, the facts were even more grim than our imaginings. I later found out about the deaths of my wife and another Jewish lady. The police told in the village how they had caught them, and both of them had requested that they be permitted to pray before being killed.

The police explained that they had killed the women first because they were drunk when they caught them, and second they themselves wanted to die, for to live longer in the forest meant hunger, dirt, and slow starvation.

There was truth in this second reason, but, oh, what difficulty I had in seeing what harm my poor, young wife had done to the Third Reich. As the days, months, and even years went by with the German occupation, and with the death penalty hanging over me as it was over all the Jews who kept on hiding from the authorities, I realized that this was the best God had for these dear ladies. They were thus spared the pain and sorrow of the remaining days and years of war.

> These are they which came out of great tribulation, and have washed their robes, and made them white in the blood of the Lamb. Therefore are they before the throne of God, and serve him day and night in his temple: and he that sitteth on the throne shall dwell among them. They shall hunger no more. . . . For the Lamb . . . shall feed them, and shall lead them unto fountains of waters; and God shall wipe away all tears from their eyes (Rev. 7:14–17).

The police pursuit quieted gradually. Night was approaching, and I realized I was safe for the time being. God wanted me to live, but for what purpose? What had happened to the others? The police had all power at their disposal. I was emaciated, clothed in old rags, and wearing boots with wooden soles. I was therefore walking and running as on stilts. Sometimes the snow would fall from one foot and I would limp until the snow from the other boot fell off too; by this time the other clean boot began to accumulate snow, and so on. It was a miracle the police had not found and killed me. But why should God want me to live?

I found a stump and sat down. After resting awhile, I gathered some dry branches, found a few matches in my pocket, and kindled a fire. If others survived the slaughter, they would see the fire and join me, or the police would come and kill me, too. I began to shout at the top of my voice. I had no desire to remain alone and regretted that I had followed my instinct to escape from death. There was no human response to my shouting. The police must have retired to the village after accomplishing their job so well. Frustrated and exhausted, I fell asleep. When I awoke, I rekindled the fire, and with dawn approaching, I began to run around in all directions looking for any human being.

There was no sense staying in the forest any longer. No bloodhound was needed to find me, as the footprints in the snow were clear. Eventually I would have to find some food. I could go immediately into the village and possibly still find the police there. Would they have pity and shoot me at once, or would they desire to take revenge for my escaping them the day before? The latter seemed more probable to me, and so I decided to leave the forest in the opposite direction. Other police would have no reason to take revenge.

When I came out of the forest, my clothes were tattered. I was cold and hungry, and I finally sought shelter with one of the peasants. This treacherous one went out quietly and brought in the village militia. I told them everything.

They bound my hands and feet and put me on a horse cart, saying they would not kill me, but had orders to deliver me to the Germans.

When I came before the German officers, they questioned me again. They decided not to kill me but to take me to a nearby slave labor camp in the village of Saycice. Here the questioning started again by the S.S. people in charge of the camp. Again they decided not to kill me but to put me to work with another large group of Jews in the camp. These people also had somehow escaped the massacres and exterminations. They were kept here to help finish the work of building a bank for the little river that ran between Chelm and this village. We were hungry, full of vermin, and always looking into the garbage cans (when the eye of the overseer was not upon us) to see if perhaps a leaf of cabbage had been thrown out from the kitchen. If so we devoured it avidly.

We were aware that our lives were spared temporarily for a reason unknown to us. Unless something unusual happened, like an armistice agreement or an exchange with one of the foreign powers, we too would be killed. Yet most of us wanted to survive.

The human desire to survive is so powerful. Truly, I could not have given a good reason for going on with my life, and the Lord knows I had many opportunities to give it up. At this point I was beginning to wonder about my own survival. How was it that I still had all my limbs and my very life? How was it that I was spared when so many of my own family and friends were exterminated? I had no answers then, but I have one now. I needed to tell this story. I needed to give the names of the forgotten ones and when they died and how they died. I needed to be able to testify that the Lord is my Shepherd and that He walked with me through the valley of death, and truly, I tell you, I feared no evil.

12

ALIVE!

The work in the camp was not too hard. At the farms we had become used to working from dawn to dusk, but now our strength was failing us. As I was new and had been hardened on farm labor, I was probably one of the strongest and best workers, and they were satisfied with me. Once when a Polish foreman noticed another laborer taking a rest, he wanted to force me to beat him up. I refused and was beaten up instead of the other. The other workers said I was lucky I was not killed for disobeying orders.

This offered a great opportunity for witness of the gospel. As a result, some of the Jewish people in this camp professed to believe that the Lord Jesus was their Savior and Messiah. Some said that perhaps the S.S. leaders in charge of the camp would give me permission to address them all as a group, but others disagreed and advised us not to stir up trouble. Unfortunately I listened to the latter, since they were in the majority.

Within a few weeks we knew that the end of this camp was at hand. The atmosphere had changed. They did not notice whether or not we worked well. We were permitted, and later commanded, to return to camp earlier each day. Each morning the bell woke us earlier than usual.

At a point when our wakeup time was about 3:00 A.M., we could discern in the shadows of the dusk the black-dressed S.S. men with their machine guns aimed at us.

Thus, the end had come for us too. How would they kill us? Would it be an easy, quick death or one of torture? Would they bury us alive or incite their dogs? Would we be taken for experiments of torture that we had heard so much about from those who temporarily escaped? Meditating on this and praying, I reached the well of the camp, where I was hoping to wash or at least wet my face. But, lo, there was no barbed wire on top of the well, for the people of the village used to come to the same well to draw water! There was no sentry watching at the well either; he had just turned his face in another direction. Why wait? If they noticed me, they would shoot at me and it would all be over quickly, with no experiments or torture. I climbed up on the well and jumped over the wall to the other side.

Again I cannot explain how, after I jumped over, they still did not notice me. Perhaps they were looking back into the camp lest there be insurrection, and never suspected that I would dare to escape.

So I was free again. I made my way into the forest, where I had hidden before. Previously I had buried two sugar beets there for an emergency; I could not eat them at that time out of sorrow for the death of my loved ones. Now I ate them. My reason returned to me, and I began to take stock of the situation.

I could well see that humanly speaking there was no possible way for me to survive. There was not even an opportunity to choose an easy or quick way to die. If I stayed in the forest, I would die of starvation, be devoured by a wild beast, or die of disease. So I collected my strength and went to my home village hoping to deliver myself to the police. The police had left my village by this time, and so I went to visit a Polish family.

I had worked many days for the man of this family and gave him all the yield of our field. He had refused to pay us anything for it, but promised that he would give us food. He did so now. The food must have been bad, however, or else I was not used to normal food. I became violently sick. Now my hope was only to reach town, give myself up, and pray that they would finish with me quickly in whatever way they wanted. I was in rags, unwashed and unshaven, and I expected to be delivered to the authorities by the first person I met, who would get a reward for delivering an escaped Jew.

But perhaps because my fear was gone, and actually I would have been glad for death, it worked the opposite way. No one paid attention to me. No one expected that a Jew would now be walking in the streets in broad daylight. As I moved along, a group of peasants going to town overtook me. I listened to their conversation for awhile and they were talking about how well the police had done their job, killing even the Jewesses who were Christians, who had prayed on their knees before they died. I realized sadly that they were talking about my wife and her friend.

When I arrived in Chelm, I had to find the Gestapo

headquarters and try to explain that I wanted to die. There was a Christian family living on the first street I came to. I decided to go in to ask the way, and perhaps also to have a word of prayer with them to encourage my spirit.

Mrs. Olichwier was recuperating from childbirth. The housemaid who was temporarily employed there brought me out some alms. I refused them and said I would like to see one of the family if at all possible. When Mrs. Olichwier saw me and finally recognized me, she began to cry, and then her husband came in. I told them that I wanted them to pray with me and direct me to the Gestapo.

Mr. Olichwier made the decision: "We will pray with you, but we will not let you go to the Gestapo." He told me that he had heard how God had delivered me in such a miraculous way, and since God wanted me to live, it would be sinful to ask for death. "How would they treat a person who had escaped them for so long?" he added to support his decision. To no avail I argued that I was dirty and perhaps too diseased to live. He prepared soap and water for me, asked me to undress and give him all my clothes. He put my filthy clothing into the fire and came back with some of his own clothing for me.

I could hardly recognize myself. My features were roughened by constant exposure to the natural elements in summer and winter. Cleaned up and wearing a peasant shirt with typical Ukrainian embroidery, I could pass for an Aryan. Also, the Nazi authorities were convinced they had done their work well and that no Aryan would dare give shelter or food to a Jewish person, and thereby risk his life. No one paid attention to us when Mr. Olichwier and

I went to church to attend the midweek prayer meeting. All of the Jews of this town were dead. The few who had escaped were soon caught and killed in one way or another. The job of extermination in our district was done completely and with precision. For awhile the authorities paid a premium for every Jew delivered to them; the captor could take all of the Jew's possessions before delivering him to the authorities. Now no one looked for a Jew. The days of bounty hunting were over.

At church Mr. Olichwier spoke to a few people about me. They advised that it would be dangerous for him to keep me in his home. One of the church members had just returned from Warsaw, and she related that there were still a few thousand Jews there who were apparently still permitted to live. They felt that if I could get to Warsaw and join them, it would be safer for me and for them. They bought me a pair of wooden-soled shoes and collected money for my train ticket to Warsaw.

It was amazing to walk the streets of Chelm without the Jewish armband or documents in my pocket and to have no one paying attention to me, no one looking deeply into my eyes to see if he could detect that I was Jewish so that he could get the price for turning me in. No one in the city knew the terrible secret that I was really Jewish, condemned to die and to be tortured for escaping. I bought my ticket and boarded the train and still no one suspected me!

I now deserved death for six separate reasons:

(1) I was a Jew.

(2) I had escaped the authorities.

(3) I was away from my place of residence.

(4) I did not wear the armband.

(5) I boarded a public train which Jews had been forbidden to do since 1939.

(6) I had no personal documents.

On the way the train was stopped, but they were not looking for Jews anymore, only for smugglers of meat. I did not have any, and they did not ask for documents. The Jews were really forgotten here.

The train arrived in Warsaw after midnight. It was after curfew, but to stay in the railway station the rest of the night would be too dangerous, as surely the police would have asked for documents. I joined the passengers who left the station. The police stopped us. I kept silent. Would they ask for documents? That would be my end. But the police did not and accepted the explanations of the other passengers and let us go. Again I was spared by a miracle.

Thus I became used to living daily by miracles. Now there was no turning back. I could not go voluntarily to the Gestapo, for they would ask who had given me food and clothing. I could not do this evil to the noble souls who had risked everything for my sake. Perhaps God would help me, and when the Gestapo caught me, I would try to escape and then be shot, before they began the torture to find the names of my benefactors.

I now had one more liability to add to all of those before. I could not even choose to give myself up. I was condemned to go on living.

When morning dawned, I went to visit my pastor, Rev. Julius Fester. He gave me food, and then informed me that I was no longer a member of this church, as they had decided to transfer all the

Jewish members to the Polish church. This they had done immediately after the German army occupied Warsaw. I was dumbfounded and did not ask him whether it was done by order of the German authorities, or whether the church had decided to be *Judenrein* (free of Jews). He told me some gruesome stories of what had happened to Jews and Hebrew Christians, but it was his opinion that since the Nazis were the government, he had to obey and remain faithful to these authorities whom God had appointed.

From there I went to the pastor of the Evangelical Christian Church, whom I had known for many years. By coincidence, the Ukrainian brother, Mr. Gryn, who now occupied the premises of the Jewish mission in Radosc, came in at the same time. The pastor asked him if he would take me in for a few days, and he agreed reluctantly. When the week was over he asked me to leave, as the neighbors were suspicious of me. Also, a man who was the sexton in the Jewish mission claimed to have recognized me from prewar years. The neighbors were afraid the authorities would burn the whole village if the truth were known.

Sunday morning came, and not knowing where to go, I went back to the German Baptist Church. Maybe I would find members who would be willing to help me. Even during the service it was difficult to understand the change that had taken place in this man of God who earlier had so faithfully preached the Word of God. Now he used the sermon to describe the victories of the Führer Hitler, and the celebrations at the Brandenburg Gate in Berlin on the occasion of the conquest of Paris.

I waited patiently until the service was over. I saw the pastor speaking to two leading members in the church. Both of them had been guest speakers at our mission to the Jewish people. They often spoke of God's election of Israel and similar themes, since they were both ardent premillennialists. It was bitter to learn of the transformation that had taken place in these men of God since I last saw them. They came and sternly forbade me ever to come into the church again. They followed me until I left the church. There were two soldiers sitting at the back. I saw one man turn to the soldiers, and I was afraid and ran away.

I spent the night in a barn on the Jewish mission property in Radosc. Again it was time to take stock of the situation. Where would I go? There was the Polish Baptist Church to which I had been transferred, but I had rarely attended it and did not know anyone there. The former pastor might have known me, but he had left prior to the war for studies in the United States. But I needed some advice as to what to do, and so I went to the Polish church.

To my great surprise, the pastor and his wife were gracious and friendly, although we were meeting for the first time. They told me that while these things were happening to me, they were in the town of Chelm for revival meetings. There they were told how God had miraculously saved me, and they wanted to do everything to help me survive. Mrs. Ivanov went to the telephone and found me a lodging place for the next few days.

I was now in an amazing situation. There seemed to be no one on earth I could trust completely. I was surrounded by my enemies, the Nazis; many of the Christians had turned away from my people; the Gentile peasants were certainly not to be trusted; and the Jews were virtually killed out to the last man. Why, I wondered, am I still alive?

13

The Handwriting
On The Wall

Pastor Ivanov was a refugee from Russia, I learned. When the Communists took over in Russia, he was a colonel in the Tsarist army. He was able to escape, as was his wife who was also a refugee. Ivanov was not a Christian in those days, but his wife was a believer, and she led him to the Lord. They were married after that but remained childless.

I told them that the brethren in Chelm actually hoped that I would be able to join the surviving Jews in the Warsaw ghetto. Of course, this wasn't easy, since the ghetto was completely walled in. Entering it was certainly as hazardous as leaving it. My friends restrained me and told me not to even think of it, for it would mean certain death. They would have liked to save all the remaining Jews in the ghetto, but they were able to bring out only one Jewish child whom they had given for adoption to a Christian family. Also they brought out a Hebrew Christian girl and arranged work for her in a home where her employers did not know that she was Jewish.

Mrs. Ivanov was able to take dramatic steps on my behalf. Since the war between Russia and Germany had broken out, she followed the lists of the Russian prisoners of war, who usually were soon exterminated in a most cruel manner as the Jews were. However, if she could prove that a prisoner was Ukrainian or White Russian, the Germans would free him. She brought back proof one day that a certain Ivan Petruschuk was White Russian, but it was too late. By the time she got his papers, the prisoner had died of starvation.

The dear Mrs. Ivanov felt that this must have been God's will and handed me Petruschuk's papers, saying, "Now you are no more Rachmiel Frydland, but Mr. Ivan Petruschuk, a White Russian."

The plan seemed preposterous to me. I pointed out to her that in the documents, the deceased one was described as being born in 1907, while I was born in 1919. She smiled sadly and assured me that I looked much older than my age, at least as old as the specification on the document. But I protested to her that the document also described a man with blond hair and I was dark-haired. She stated that I could apply some peroxide to my hair and be a convincing blond.

Considering the circumstances, it was not a bad idea. If I held an Aryan document, I was certainly an easier person to help than if I were a known Jew. If people gave me shelter and were later apprehended for it, they could claim that I had shown my papers and they had no idea that I was Jewish. As to how I would get my food, Mrs. Ivanov could only advise me to return to my village and see if the peasants would pay me a little for my labor and for the house and furniture that they took over.

Thus, at Christmastime, 1942, I reached my village again. The people did not want to give me money, but the friendly ones gave much food. Early Christmas morning I made my way back to Chelm, hoping to take the train at night back to Warsaw. On the way I was caught.

A local soldier recognized me and there was no point in pleading with him. In a few minutes he would contact the Gestapo, and my fate would be sealed. Worse, they would want to know who gave me food and shelter, and most certainly how I obtained the false document. I tried not to panic.

As he led me into the town toward the Gestapo headquarters, I said simply, "I am going to be killed anyway. You know of my belief in the Lord Jesus, and since I may not have another chance, I will kneel down here in the street and pray for you and for me before I die. You may beat me, kill me, or do whatever you like."

My captor softened up after prayer and began to talk to me. He wanted all the money I had. I was glad to give it to him. Then he turned away and went back to his home, leaving me standing speechless.

What a Christmas that was! I returned to Warsaw without incident, moment by moment kept alive solely by the grace of God.

My greatest problem was to find people who would let me spend a night or two in their homes. It was impossible to remain in the streets because of the curfew. Death was certain if I did not find shelter, but what right had I to make others risk their lives? In the daytime I could sit in the Roman Catholic or Protestant cemeteries and spend my hours in meditation. In the winter months I could sit in the Roman Catholic Church which was open for mass and prayers at least until noontime. But where would I go for the night?

In desperation I tried to leave Warsaw and go back to Plock. Perhaps the brethren would help me and I would again find work on the farms. Unfortunately the trip meant crossing the new border between the General Government and the German Reich, and I was caught again.

This time I ran for it through a hail of bullets. By God's grace my tormentors were unable to kill me. The bullets whizzed by me on all sides and as I ran I breathed thanks to the Lord.

I arrived again in the city, by this time completely counting on the reliable help of God. It was winter, and I knew that the Lord would help me to find some shelter.

There was another pastor in the city whom I had known previously. He had attended Bible school in the United States and had married an American girl, and now he was pastor of an Evangelical Christian church on Pulawska Street in Warsaw. His church was on the border between the German and the Polish districts. To keep his church intact he had to take in people of German nationality. By God's leading he found a seventy-year-old German Christian woman, Mrs. Keiming, a nurse who lived in the church apartment. The pastor and his family moved to a suburb, and thus he could come to church, attend to the business, and maintain contact with the believers. He told the nurse that I was a needy person and asked her to prepare some food for me and let me spend the night in the church premises. She looked at me suspiciously, but finally agreed. What a meal it was, with good fresh vegetables, such as I had not eaten for a long time. Because she was of German nationality, she received better rations and fresh vegetables.

I slept at the church and the next morning was asked by Mrs. Keiming where I intended to spend the following night. What answer could I give? She told me to come back if I did not find any other place. Since I rarely found another place, I kept coming back just a few minutes before curfew and leaving before daybreak, but this also had to come to an end.

Mrs. Keiming became more restless. The neighbors hinted that they suspected me, and yet she had not the heart to send me out in the street. She told me she was not sleeping well at night because she was in fear. One night she heard the German police with their loud swearing. She was sure they were coming for me, so she sent me out to the fire escape. As it was night, no one saw me on the staircase. This would certainly have been the end of me.

Even as this place was partly closing up for me, God was opening another door, the store of Mr. Jacyszyn. Before the war he was a laborer but he also did some carpentry. Since he was of Ukrainian nationality, he was given privileges like those given to people of German nationality. As the Jewish people of the ghetto were exterminated, their houses and stores became ownerless. These were now given to people of German nationality or to ones whom they considered to be their allies. Thus Mr. Jacyszyn got his store free of charge. The Jews who were still alive came out of the ghetto by special permit and did the work, cleaning and renovating these properties. They were happy to be out of the ghetto at least during the daytime.

Mr. Jacyszyn went into business as an undertaker, making his own coffins since he was a carpenter. Business was good, needless to say. The enormous death rate in Poland still did not provide many lucrative opportunities for a coffin maker, of course, but there were people who wanted to be buried well and had the means.

The undertaker let another Hebrew Christian man and me sleep in the coffins at night. The irony of the situation was not lost on me; here I was, alive only by a series of intricate miracles, retiring every night already prepared for my burial.

My companion was not satisifed with the coffin arrangements and went instead to a Jewish woman living with false identity papers in a Warsaw hotel. Soon he was spotted as a Jew and the two of them were killed by the authorities. I expected the same fate under the circumstances, and so retired each night to my strange but appropriate sleeping quarters.

I found out from the Jews who had special permits to leave the ghetto each day that some of the Hebrew Christians were still alive. Since so few souls were left in the ghetto, they knew one another well. I asked the Jewish man in charge of the working group whether he could bring me into the ghetto and put me in touch with the Hebrew Christians.

It might be thought extraordinary that I should try to inflitrate *into* the Warsaw Ghetto when people were giving their lives to try to get *out* of it. But in my state of mind it seemed a reasonable move. I was surely going to die at any moment. Why should I not die with my own people?

The foreman of the working group agreed, and the next Friday, instead of taking out ten Jews on his permit, he took only nine and brought me back into the ghetto as the tenth.

I put on the Jewish armband and felt at rest among my people.

In the ghetto I met the magnificent saint, Stasiek Eisenberg. He was one of our Hebrew Christian young men who had procrastinated about his baptism, although he had received the Lord in the mission. In the ghetto he got in touch with Pastor Krakiewicz, who received special permission to enter the ghetto for a few hours to baptize him there.

Stasiek had a long story to tell me. He related how some of the Hebrew Christians had died of starvation. Among them was the family of Mr. Weiss, a missionary for the Church Mission to the Jews (C.M.J.),[1] and Joseph Sommer, one of the greatest Hebrew Christian scholars in Rabbinics. His wife had survived and married a non-Jew, having somehow obtained Aryan identity papers. Mr. Schuman, when hunger pressured him and his family, posed as a German and asked a Jewish manufacturer to give him some money. The latter called the police and they arrested and killed him. Later they came for Mr. Schuman's family. Some of the members of his family could have saved themselves, but they preferred to die together—Mrs. Schuman, her son, two daughters, a son-in-law, and the tiny grandchild. As

[1]Now called the Church Ministry to the Jews.

to Mr. and Mrs. Sendyk, under whom I worked in the mission, their boy Heniek was killed by the authorities. Neither did they try to hide or save their own lives, but went freely when the authorities came to take them away for extermination.

The only Hebrew Christians still alive in the ghetto were Stasiek Eisenberg and Mr. and Mrs. Wolfin. Mr. Wolfin was the most outstanding preacher of the C.M.J. Mission on Severinov Street. He was learned in Rabbinics, but with his blond moustache, he did not look Jewish. He was often able to sneak out of the ghetto and contact Christian families. He asked them to shelter his wife for the duration of the war. Since he could not find a Christian family willing to take the risk, he stayed with his wife in the small ghetto awaiting final extermination.

Stasiek himself was deeply aware of God's presence and ability to save to the uttermost, physically and spiritually. Once he was arrested for being late to work, and for this he was condemned to die. In the death cell everyone wrote something on the wall. He wrote in Polish the first verse of his favorite hymn, *"Niechaj w sercach radosc plonie,"* which is in English translation:

> Let your hearts be always joyful. Praise and thank Him without fears.
> For our Father in the Heavens,
> On His arm His children bears.
> Joyful, joyful, always joyful,
> Day by day His sun doth shine;
> Full of beauty is the road to Heaven,
> God and Christ are always mine.

The following day the officer in charge came in with his Polish interpreter. He wanted him to translate the writings on the wall, a thing that had never been done before. The Polish interpreter did his best, but it was only similar to the original German of this hymn. The officer stopped him before he finished and asked, "Who wrote this?" With trembling Stasiek came forward. Everyone thought his turn had come to be killed. Instead he was freed the same day!

Apparently the officer recognized his Sunday school hymn in the original German.

But now Stasiek waited pointlessly in the small ghetto with death seeming near. He was in touch with the Jewish underground and had reliable information that within a few days the police would kill the rest of the Jews. The young people prepared to resist in desperation, knowing full well that they could do little against a power that had conquered almost all of Europe. Many of the older people were carrying cyanide to poison themselves instead of being killed in cruel manners by the S.S. Stasiek wanted to know whether he, as a Christian, could join the underground or carry the cyanide poison in his pocket. He wanted to know what was happening outside. Were Christians really singing and rejoicing as though nothing had happened, while cruel Nazis committed atrocities such as dashing babies against the walls, or throwing them from an upper room for another soldier to catch on his bayonet—just for fun.

To these and other questions he put to me, I had no answers. I too was a new believer and was not able to decide for him, so I just listened. Then I told him of the decision I had made to stay with him and with the Jewish people in the ghetto. He did not even want to listen but adjured me not to stay any longer. "Our days are numbered," he said. "There is no escape from here."

He felt that since God had kept me safe for such a long time outside the ghetto, He wanted me to live. Perhaps I was the one destined to tell the story of the Jewish Christians who perished at the hands of people who considered themselves a Christian nation. I was now vaguely beginning to understand God's insistence that I survive. "I alone am left to tell thee," I would sadly say someday outside that horrible ghetto.

I asked if Stasiek would join me in living outside the ghetto, but he felt that his features were too Jewish. He could not exist as I had, by day in cemeteries, churches, or traveling aimlessly, and by night without a sure shelter. He would be soon recognized and made to give an account of how he escaped. If a Christian family could be found to hide him, he would be grateful. Otherwise he preferred to die with the Jewish people.

At midnight, when the new shift left the ghetto to work in one of the German factories, I made my move. I had joined the workers, but as soon as we were outside the ghetto, I took off the blue and white armband and separated from them. It was after curfew, but I was near the undertaker's store. I climbed over the fence and spent the rest of the night in the outside lavatory, waiting for the opening of the store.

14

"... Of Whom The World Was Not Worthy."

Stasiek, like an Old Testament prophet, had known only too well what was to come to pass. The next weekend the ghetto was a wall of flames. The few thousand Jews who remained decided to resist the Nazi armies that had come to exterminate them with tanks and airplanes. The cowardly assault continued as the Germans even brought up siege guns, as though they were facing a formidable enemy. The nearly unarmed Jews defended themselves, hiding often even in sewer pipes and, though the outcome was certain, they were able to inflict heavy casualties on their exterminators. The Germans who attacked the Warsaw ghetto saw a display of valor that was to haunt them long after the war.

Stasiek and Mr. and Mrs. Wolfin were killed, as so many Hebrew Christians had been previously. Outside the ghetto the situation became even more dangerous, since some Jews had abandoned the burning ghetto territory and were on the loose in the city. Again those who hated us began to look everyone in the eyes to detect Jewish features or fears and to deliver such to the Gestapo, hoping for a reward. It was more difficult to find shelter, and I had many narrow escapes. From day to day as these things happened, the assurance grew that perhaps after all I was destined to survive to tell this story.

With the destruction of the ghetto and continued Allied victories, the hunt for Jews stopped again. Many of the non-Jewish people were now ashamed that such cruelties had happened in their country. The Jewish man who brought me into the ghetto and had arranged for me to meet Stasiek had somehow gotten free of the ghetto. He had been a rich builder in prewar days, and so he had many contacts with Polish families who took him in and gave him shelter.

He and I spent some time together and he came to at least a mental belief in the Lord Jesus as the Messiah. But in 1944, when the Russian army approached Warsaw, he was hiding with a peasant just outside the city, and he could hide no longer. He carried a sheaf of wheat on his head as a sort of camouflage, and began to run toward the Russian positions, seeing the advancing Russians as his deliverers from the Nazis.

The Germans called him to stop, but he kept on running and they shot and killed him.

Toward the end of the war I led almost a normal life. I found that a Seventh Day Adventist church in Warsaw had their meetings on Saturdays and it was another safe place to spend the day. So each Saturday morning I was there before the church opened and stayed until after the evening service. This meant one full day of shelter each week.

The pastor realized my need and introduced me to one of his members who could help me. This man was in touch with the Polish underground and was able to take a photograph of me and obtain a valid-looking identity card bearing my picture and my new Gentile name. My new credential seemed more valid, of course, but if the police caught me and checked the records, they would still kill me because my real name was not on the card. Besides, each person was now required to have an employment card, along with an identity card. However, people who now gave me shelter could reasonably claim that they had taken in a bona fide Aryan with at least one document to prove it.

Soon another door opened for me. A Christian lady asked me to care for her son who had suffered a mental breakdown. He was being treated at home, of course, since the Nazis had killed all the mentally sick in the hospitals. The mother was a concert pianist in prewar days, but now earned her living by giving lessons. Thus she still occupied her plush apartment in Warsaw. But she did not have money to pay for fuel, so during the day we three stayed in one little room. At night I was grateful to have even an unheated room to sleep in. Her son improved with insulin treatment, and at a certain point my services were no longer needed. However, the mother's brother had come often to visit her, and he asked if I would like to work with him on his small vegetable and fruit farm just outside the city. He could not pay, but would provide food and lodging. It was certainly a wonderful opportunity for me. In the pastoral suburbs of Warsaw no one would suspect that a Jew was still alive. Thus, Mr. Koziol, my new employer, though not a Christian, was surely a Godsend.

This was the time of great Soviet victories in the war. The Russians already had recaptured all Soviet territory and were now in Poland, moving gradually toward Warsaw. At the end of the summer of 1944 two Soviet tanks came into our village but immediately withdrew. Then German authorities ordered the civilian population to be evacuated.

In Warsaw proper there was an insurrection against the Germans, and I certainly had to stay away from it. I made my way to Wisniewo, a suburb north of the city. There were a few Christian families here, and they wanted to have Christian services every evening, praying especially for the population of Warsaw.

Warsaw was aflame night after night, and as we looked on the bright sky from our windows, we thought nothing could be left of this great city. Indeed, the German army crushed the insurrection with fire and blood, while the Soviet tanks were several miles away and did not interfere.

As the winter of 1944 approached, our small Christian community was more or less caught on the open battlefield. Soviet tanks were pressing us from the east, and the Germans desperately dug in on the west. I tried to stay hidden with the other young Christians, so as not to be evacuated by the German overlords and thus discovered as a Jew. However, the Germans moved into our territory and chased us out. They were not the S.S. and, distracted by the Russian advance, had lost interest in killing civilians.

My work now in Wisniewo was with a family by the name of Hankiewicz. I helped Mr. Hankiewicz in all the work around the house so that he had more time for his trade of butchering animals and making sausages. Their son had been taken to work on a farm in Germany, and so they had me take over his chores. But the Germans moved us out of the contested area to a little village some twenty miles west of Warsaw, close to the textile town of Zyrardow.

In this village we tried to interest the people, who were Roman Catholic, with the gospel. We had nightly meetings for them, but we ourselves needed fellowship with other Christians. On Sunday morning we made our way to Zyrardow, some ten miles away, to look for believers. We formed a little congregation, and although the Christians knew I was Jewish, they asked me to preach every Sunday morning. The S.S. and the Gestapo had already withdrawn. The Soviets were knocking at the gates of Warsaw, and now no one was looking for Jews, or suspecting one another. I was able to earn a little money for my benefactors and me, as I carried Mr. Hankiewicz's sausages and sold them in Zyrardow. Of course, the death penalty on Jews was not lifted, and anyone could still accuse me before the authorities, but even then they would not take time to torture me but would probably quickly finish with me. Death, my constant companion, held little fear for me anymore.

But instead the unforgettable day came when the death penalty for being a Jew was lifted. I was no longer condemned to die! It was the seventh anniversary of my baptism, January 15, 1945, when I could walk about as a free man. It seemed to me that I had lived several lifetimes by then. I felt like an old man, but in reality I was only twenty-five.

The once proud and haughty German army fled in panic as Polish and Soviet troops swept through the land. I returned immediately to Warsaw to see if any of my sisters or relatives survived, but none were there.

When I set out at night to make my way to Chelm to see if I could find any of my relatives, I did not realize that the main bridge on the Vistula was bombed out. As I reached the middle of the bridge, I suddenly came to a precipice! Returning, I sought another way over the river, fell into a bombed-out hole, and almost broke my leg.

But I laughed off these small tribulations. Imagine! The death penalty for being a Jew was lifted and I could walk around like a normal human being!

In Chelm and in my own village I found none of my relatives alive. They had all been killed. I alone of my family survived. Moshe-Yoseph's grandson, who was taken on the death march in the beginning of the war, somehow made it all the way to Russia, and he also came to look for relatives. But none of his family had survived either.

Moshe-Yoseph's grandson and I, of course, had something in common now, as lone survivors. While in Russia he became a Communist, and so we had some interesting discussions. He was open to the gospel and at least admitted that Communism in Russia did not work as it ought to and it needed reform.

The Polish Evangelical Baptist Church invited me to work for them as an itinerant preacher. This was of great help to my spiritual and physical rehabilitation. It brought me in contact with many pastors and from them I heard the stories of other Hebrew Christians who had died and remained faithful to the very end. Some of these families were well known to me. When the time came for them to face death, they prepared their children, partook of the Lord's Supper with them, told them not to be afraid and that the pain would last only a few minutes. Then they would be in a better place, a mansion in heaven. The children sometimes had given their testimonies to the exterminators and had died without hate in full reconciliation with God through Christ Jesus. There they rest even now in the unknown graves of Poland and western Russia with no one molesting them anymore. But God spared them the tribulations that we who had survived went through. No more are they with us—those dear ones, my friends—Mr. Mandelbaum, Mr. and Mrs. Leibovich with their little children, Mr. and Mrs. Soffer with their five little children, Mr. Mehlsack, and many others . . .

> . . . of whom the world was not worthy. . . . For this we say unto you by the word of the Lord, that we which are alive and remain unto the coming of the Lord shall not prevent them which are asleep. . . . The dead in Christ shall rise first: Then we which are alive and remain shall be caught up together with them in the clouds, to meet the Lord in the air: and so shall we ever be with the Lord (Heb. 11:38; 1 Thess. 4:15–17).

15

The Heart
Is Deceitful

Though I was no longer condemned to death for being Jewish, there were now new dangers on every side. There was a local war between the Polish nationalists and those who were coworking with the Communist regime. No sooner had the Nazi occupation finished, than the Communist occupation began. The people of Poland had had enough occupation of any sort, and many of them had regrouped to fight the Communists.

I was now walking or traveling by horse cart from village to village to preach the gospel, and it happened one day that I was ironically brought again to the point of death, this time not for being Jewish, but for being a suspected Communist. I was in the company of an older believer who, because of his Russian background, was wearing a white patriarchal beard. We were detained by nationalist troops who demanded to know if we were Jewish Communists. We denied it, of course, but I had Jewish Bibles with me and my brother in Christ was suspected of being a Jew because of his beard. It was no longer illegal to be Jewish, strictly speaking, but it was not a good thing either.

The soldiers were going to kill us, but they decided

at length that they would simply hold us until they inquired about our true political leanings. They confiscated our documents and all of our possessions and went to their headquarters to check on us. Three men remained with us and held their guns pointed at us. After midnight the others returned and all was well. They accompanied us to the next village and told us never to come back or tell anyone about their outpost.

I established contact with the Mildmay Mission to the Jews, for whom I had worked until the outbreak of World War II. They again began to send me money. Others in America and elsewhere sent me food parcels and clothing. I found my brother-in-law, Meir Panaczuk, who survived the war but was now remarried. He told me how my sister in Lodz and their two children were separated from him in the Auschwitz Concentration Camp. They were taken immediately to the extermination chambers, while he was kept alive to work. He was liberated by the Allied armies and was now planning to go to Israel.

Life slowly came back to normal for me, despite the ultimate Communist takeover. New chapters of my life were to open up as the Lord led me out of Poland. But I cannot leave my story of the war without presenting certain conclusions that came into my heart through all of these bitter experiences, although I do not mean to sound like some sage or philosopher. The lessons I had learned about man and his behavior made these realizations crystal clear to me:

1. The war definitely taught me anew the truth of

the well-known verse in Jeremiah 17:9, "The heart is deceitful above all things, and desperately wicked: who can know it?" It is as true in the twentieth century A.D. as it was in Jeremiah's time, the seventh century B.C., when these words were uttered. Possibly all men, even so-called Christians and churchgoers, are capable of all cruelties, but in wartime such behavior comes into the open.

2. I believe Christians should be prepared for a time like this. Our churches stress the obligation to obey the powers that are ordained under God according to Romans 13. Should we not also be taught that there are times when a Christian is obliged to disobey his leaders and the laws of his own country? The pastor and members of the German Baptist Church were probably born-again Christians. However, their government made these laws, and therefore, they reasoned, they must obey them. When they were ordered to expel all Hebrew Christian members from their churches they obeyed, thinking they were thereby fulfilling the Scriptures. In Hitler they saw the only leader who truly resisted Communism. If he said that all Jews were bad and should be exterminated like vermin, they thought they were transgressing God's Word if they disobeyed the power appointed by God.

This was true not only of the German Christians. I can still see in my mind the puzzled face of the deacon in the Polish Evangelical Christian Church as he said, "You come to me to help you, to give you food or shelter, but I will be transgressing the laws of my country which I am commanded in the Word of God to obey." Upon this, he showed me the

Scriptures of Jeremiah 29:7 and Romans 13:1–7. At that time I had nowhere to go and so I stayed for the church service. He spoke on these texts to show that we have to be obedient also to the Nazi authorities. Many Christians had helped me until that time, and I knew that the ones who helped me were right and he was wrong. However, I was a young Christian and he was an elder, a deacon and a preacher, and who was I to contradict his teaching?

On the other hand, there were Christians like the brave Mrs. Ivanov. Because of her resistance to government decrees, at least five Hebrew Christians survived the massacres. Two of us are in the Lord's service. She saved a certain little girl from the burning Warsaw ghetto and found a Christian home for her. After the war this girl moved to Russia and there received the Lord Jesus as her personal Savior. She was active in the church in Rovno and was a bright shining light in dark, Red Soviet Russia. Her father survived the war and recently in 1969 they found one another. She is now trying to win her father to faith in the Lord Jesus. In Denmark the whole Jewish population was saved from certain death because the Christians decided to resist the authorities and smuggle the Jews out of Denmark into neutral Sweden. In Holland a large segment of the Jewish population was saved from death and many of them have become born-again Christians and are serving the Lord because the Christians understood the Scriptures differently than the deacon in Poland.

3. The German and Polish Christians lacked teaching in the Word of God, and therefore did not act in

uniformity. Hebrew Christians also did not act in uniformity, possibly because we also did not know the Word of God. Those who were more spiritual, closer to the Lord, did not seek shelter nor try to escape, nor did they offer any resistance. They immediately obeyed government orders, offering themselves to the German Gestapo to be killed in various ways with their wives and children. Was I wrong in escaping and trying to hide? I never knew for certain whether I did the right thing, but once I started to hide and find shelter with Christians, I had to continue because of the danger to my benefactors. Those who led us to Christ did not teach us how to behave in a situation like this!

4. Between five and six million Jews were killed in the six-year war. Some were tortured in the cruelest ways that the perversity of man invented. Many were shot and buried still alive, but most died in the gas chambers in the various concentration camps—gas chambers which were invented by the ingenuity of modern science and installed for that purpose by a nation that called itself Christian, with the majority of its population Protestant.

If Hitler was a type of the Antichrist, then we have full proof that even some of the "elect" can blindly follow such a leader to kill, pillage, and destroy innocent people, merely because the leader says they are guilty. The young people who joined the S.S. troops fell away from the church and some began to make fun of Jesus and Mary, the Jew and the Jewess. The older Christians did not see the writing on the wall but continued to give physical and moral support to Hitler and his sytem.

5. Maybe it is unfair and impetuous to condemn the majority of the German Christians who lived in Poland. I can only say with John Bradford, "There but for the grace of God goes Rachmiel Frydland." Had I been born of German parents in Poland, I probably also would have followed the policies of my government, even if it included pillage, destruction, and extermination of millions of people; especially if my government explained that it was done to save the world from "Jewish Communism." Only by the grace of God was I born a Jew, to be persecuted and not to have had the opportunity to persecute others. Who can know the heart of man, even my own heart? He that stands, let him watch lest he falls. I have not written this to condemn but to warn others as well as myself.

6. I needed to know how to apply God's Word to these unusual events as much as did other Gentile and Hebrew Christians. Even the term "Hebrew Christian" was not well defined for me. To the first Nazi who asked me, "Are you a Jew?" I showed my certificate of baptism and membership in a Christian church. Subconsciously I hoped that I would thereby temporarily avoid the sufferings and humiliations of my brethren after the flesh. I was probably wrong in doing this, but I was never taught how to behave in such exceptional circumstances.

Since that time, I never again attempted to find mercy or favor because I was a Christian. I wore the Star of David armband to show the world I was Jewish, lived under the same humiliations and restrictions as other Jewish people as long as they permitted us to live, ran away to escape death as did some other young Jews. While knowing that I was a believer in Christ and a member of a Christian church, the Jewish people treated me with love and compassion as they would one another in such circumstances. Yet we somehow must have failed our own Jewish brethren since now that the persecutions are ended, many of them consider us Hebrew Christians as non-Jews, apostates, and traitors! Why should they treat us differently now after we have survived the cruel war?

7. Though so many Jews were killed—more than half of them in Poland—when a Christian decided to disobey the law of extermination and took in a Jewish child, man, or woman, to give shelter, God honored that willingness of obedience and sacrifice. As far as I know, none of the Christians in Poland who sheltered Jewish people was ever caught or killed (although after the war I heard that there were some such cases in Holland).

The only exceptions would be the Wisniewski family, members of the Polish Baptist Church. Mr. and Mrs. Wisniewski were about seventy-five years old. They and their son, Jan, about fifty years old, died of typhoid. It was rumored that they got the disease via a Jewish Christian boy, Edelstein by name. His parents, who were Hebrew Christians, had been killed, but he was left alive and was seeking shelter among the Polish Christians. The Wisniewskis took him in for a few nights, and then after a few days they became frightened and told him not to return. He went out into the streets, was caught after curfew, and killed. He did not give out who his benefactors were, and he is now forever with the Lord, as is the Wisniewski family who helped him out for a few days. Their reward is great in heaven and it has never been proved that it was this boy who brought the typhoid germ of which this dear family died.

When Christians helped Jewish children consistently, both the children and their benefactors usually survived. In most cases the Jewish children were led to a personal knowledge of the Lord Jesus, and later married and established Christian homes in Poland, Scotland, Holland, the United States, Israel, and wherever the Lord led and scattered them as witnesses to their own brethren after the flesh. What if there had been more such Christian families who loved the Lord and would have been willing to shelter these who were persecuted, and to "rescue the perishing, care for the dying, snatch them in pity from death and the grave"? It would have been life instead of death for thousands of other Jewish people, and perhaps history itself would have taken another course.

What will happen next time should similar things occur? Will we be ready and willing?

16

Festivals Of Thanksgiving

When all fighting in Poland had ceased, I traveled throughout the land still looking for some survivors of my family, or close friends, Jewish and Hebrew Christians. I finally determined for certain that none of my immediate family had survived.

My brother-in-law who had survived Auschwitz told me the bitter story of how my oldest sister and her two children were killed. My younger sister, my grandmother, my uncles, and the rest of my relatives who were in Warsaw must have perished together with the half-million Jews who lived in that city, but no one knew any facts. The Hebrew Christians who survived were those who escaped to foreign countries, and a few who had married non-Jewish women were somehow preserved by them.

All of the leading Hebrew Christians—missionaries, pastors, teachers, scholars—who remained in Poland perished. I knew that I owed my life to God, who had so miraculously and exceptionally spared me, but what was I to do now? The Communist government in Poland did not bother me, except that they questioned me intensely about my contacts with the West. The president of the Polish Baptist Church offered me a pastorate in a newly annexed city in the west of Poland. But how could I pastor others when I had just emerged from such a nightmare of death and had not as yet found my bearings?

About this time two representatives of the Mildmay Mission to the Jews, Rev. Charles Fisher and Rev. H. E. Ellison came to visit me in Poland. They probably expected that I would reestablish a Jewish work, but I was not as yet capable of this. They asked me what else I could do, and I answered that I wanted to go to a Bible school since I never had received the basic Christian education needed for the Lord's work. They thereupon sent a cable to the All Nations Bible College in England, asking them to receive me as a student. I was accepted by return cable and then received an official letter of acceptance.

It took more than seven months, with an endless number of certificates for tax payment, military exemption, police record, church affiliation, and so forth, until the necessary passport was handed to me. I arrived only two days late for the beginning of the school term in October, 1947.

I studied avidly. Many years had passed since my mental development was arrested in such a cruel way, and I took to the books like a thirsty person at a water fountain. The Bible college studies were not enough for me, and I found that I could study for the London University entrance examinations as an additional challenge. Then I began to study for the bachelor's degree, which at that time in London was based mostly on classical and European languages. Because I had a good background in languages, it was not difficult for me to get a B.A. degree with honors in biblical languages. As time went on, I also obtained the B.D. and the M.A. degrees from London University and later on the M.A. degree from New York University.

Questions still remained with me: What was the meaning of this long nightmare for our people? Was it all in vain? This could not be, I reasoned, since I had so many tokens of God's presence and intervention in my own life and in the history of my people. Was it for the punishment of our sins? But did the poverty-stricken Jews in Poland commit more sins than the almost godless and affluent Jews of the West? Yet those were not killed. Perhaps the Western Jews were saved from physical death not because of their own merits, but because of Western Christianity, which was less degenerate than ours. In the West the Christians practiced what they preached and were ready to fight and die, not only for their own country but to save the remnant of Jews in Europe. If my people had known the things that pertain to their salvation, namely, to believe in the Lord Jesus and to proclaim Him to the people in Poland and the rest of Eastern Europe, this disaster would never have happened.

Yet there was fruit from the blood of the Jewish martyrs. There was the national and physical revival of Israel. The Lord had permitted Israel to be smitten by the heathen and now He offered the hand of reconciliation through the Gentiles. It was as if the nations suddenly realized they had exceeded the measure of their wickedness toward our people, and in repentance voted a home for Israel in her own land. Thus they contributed to the fulfillment of prophecies that speak of Israel's return to her borders. As it is written:

> If any of thine be driven out unto the outmost parts of heaven, from thence will the Lord thy God gather thee, and from thence will he fetch thee (Deut. 30:4).

There must also be a spiritual significance to all these things that had happened, and I was reminded of the Scripture in Romans 2:4:

> Or despisest thou the riches of his goodness and forbearance and longsuffering; not knowing that the goodness of God leadeth thee to repentance?

Perhaps God is now dealing with Israel in the same manner. First by severity and sufferings and now by His goodness. He is encouraging the Gentile nations to help Israel regather the Jewish dispersion to their own land.

I graduated from All Nations Bible College and received my first degree from London University. And now the call came to work in the metropolis of New York with its three million Jewish people.

I had the privilege of crossing the Atlantic on the stately H.M.S. *Queen Elizabeth*. While aboard the ship, I feasted on rich foods that simply amazed me, and I took every opportunity of explaining to my fellow passengers my purpose in going to the United States. I had many chances to explain the gospel of salvation.

An American on the ship tried to explain the holiday of Thanksgiving to me since we were to arrive on the eve of this celebration, November 26, 1952, but I frankly understood little of its significance

I will never forget my first impression of America as our ship drew near the Statue of Liberty and we gazed at the awesome skyscrapers of Manhattan. They were so much greater and mightier than I had ever dreamed of—what wonderful wisdom and grandeur God has imparted to man for human beings to build such monumental edifices, I thought.

The ship was met by several people of Hermon House, the society who had invited me to the United States, including the director, Solomon Birnbaum. Dr. Birnbaum had been a former professor at Moody Bible Institute and head of the department of Jewish studies. He kindly extended an invitation to his home for the festival of Thanksgiving, but we meanwhile partook of a wonderful meal in the east end of Manhattan, where a fine corned beef sandwich at Katz's Delicatessen cost less than fifty cents. Dr. Birnabaum filled me in on the Jewish situation in New York, and I was amazed to learn that every third person in that great city was Jewish.

Our mission in that time was simply approaching the Jewish people with Messianic literature. We moved from one building to another and talked with our brethren about faith in Jesus Christ. The stories of salvation are legion and would by themselves make a book this size. Representative perhaps is the testimony of the victorious and patient Manuel Schnall, who actually sought us out. Manual had come through many tribulations. Both his parents had died, his sister had drifted into sin, and he was seeking some reasonable way of life. I invited him to stay with me at Hermon House (our mission's headquarters), as he had no home at that time. (It was now my privilege to offer other people a room for the night!)

Manuel, who was in his late teens, was bright, hard working, and knew several languages, including Yiddish and some Hebrew. He studied hard, cleaned my rooms, and began looking for a job. At length he found a position in a Jewish nursing home where he joyously performed the menial tasks of washing, shaving, and cleaning the old men in his care, usually carrying them to the washrooms and back. He accepted the Lord Jesus, and great was his joy when old Mr. Sam Forman, a Jewish believer in Jesus, came to stay in the same nursing home. Mr. Forman had constantly attended our meetings. He knew the Jewish Talmud and the Messianic prophecies in Hebrew by heart, with their rabbinic interpretations. Now both of them, so old and so young, had a grand time celebrating together the heavenly language of Messiah Yeshua. Manuel wanted to fulfill the Messiah's command of immersion and asked me to perform it. On a cool autumn morning we went to Coney Island in Brooklyn, New York. We put on the robes, prayed, read the Scriptures, and Manuel had the fulfillment of his heart's desire—he was baptized in Messiah's death to arise a victorious believer in Messiah Jesus.

Now there was a Jewish young lady who came to know the Lord in Bridgeport, Connecticut. Somehow Manuel and Ida found out about one another. Ida too had lost her parents. She had been working for her brothers who had a store, but they sold out and moved to Florida. Ida and Manuel met, fell in love, and were married. This is not the end of the story, for Manual is now holding my former position as Secretary for the International Hebrew Christian Alliance in Israel (I.H.C.A.).

I received a call one day from a certain Mrs. Moss, whose mother had taken an apparently fatal fall. The frail old lady was not expected to live out the day, and the family was hurrying to the home of Mrs. Moss to prepare her funeral. I got to the house as quickly as I could, finding the old lady alive but very much in pain. I spoke consolingly to her and told her that God was able to heal her, but pointed out the system of sacrifices in the Old Testament and that we each need an atonement; and how God wonderfully provided such an atonement as described in Isaiah 53. Her eyes shown with faith and I prayed with her the sinner's prayer. I also prayed in the name of the Lord that this dear old one be healed. I had only just completed my prayers when Mrs. Moss came in to tell us that the relatives had arrived for the funeral. Well, the old lady was not ready to die and informed all of her sons and relatives that she had been healed by the Savior. They could see it was true and they all left presently. I visited with the old lady a few years later and she was still in fine health, deeply enjoying her relationship with the Lord Jesus.

I ministered gladly in New York City, but my true heart's desire and prayer, like Paul's, was for the salvation of Israel (see Rom. 10:1). In 1961 God opened the way for me. The International Hebrew Christian Alliance asked me to go to the Promised

Land. They were seeking to unite the Jewish believers in Christ throughout the world without respect to denominations and to encourage them to witness to their Jewish brethren.

I arrived in Haifa on the same boat with Jewish emigrants from Poland, Morocco, Rumania, Russia, and many other parts of the world. Israel was now their home. Some of them had tried hard to conform to the culture and habits of their countries, but they had to endure anti-Semitic outbreaks. Now they reached the shore where the word "Jew" is the nicest thing you can say about a person instead of being a curse. This magic word "Jew" opens all doors. Automatically they have a home, a job, immediate citizenship of Israel, and help in every other way—just because one is a Jew. What a welcome change from my previous experience!

The boat reached Haifa on the eve of Israel's anniversary of independence. God always seems to bring me to countries I have never been to before during great festivals of thanksgiving. The city of Haifa was nearly deserted as everyone streamed to Jerusalem to see the military parade. I joined the crowd and found a bus that was leaving late at night for the celebrations. We could not get lodging in Jerusalem because of the crowds, but with other people I strolled to the center of the city and walked about the streets waiting for daybreak. I was certainly a veteran in passing long nights in the darkness, but what a difference from Warsaw!

In the morning I found hospitality with Jewish believers. The Israeli heavy tanks were hidden, but were not far away, in case the kingdom of Jordan might make trouble. But the Jordanians held their peace. Masses of Jewish people lined the streets and balconies cheered the valiant Israeli soldiers and their weapons.

But my heart was a bit heavy. Our people are much preoccupied with these temporal things as they were so long without a land and without military might. There is little left in the heart of Israel for anything else. Our people seem to have forgotten the words of the Torah and the prophets, saying, "Man doth not live by bread only" (Deut. 8:3), and, "Not by might, nor by power, but by my spirit, saith the Lord of hosts" (Zech. 4:6). At the same time I found much comfort in the Word of God which says: "Even so then at this present time also there is a remnant according to the election of grace" (Rom. 11:5).

This remnant among the Jewish people is at the present time scattered all over Israel, and I was soon to meet them one by one and in groups. How many are there in this small remnant? Perhaps three hundred, just as many as Gideon of old had with him in Judges 7:6. There were Jewish immigrants and Israeli citizens in all walks of life who believed in the Lord Jesus Christ. Some of them had positions with the military authorities, one dealt in classified material, another worked with Shin-Bet, Israel's intelligence and security forces. There were physicians, dentists, students, a jailor, and a police officer. The majority, however, were the poor, humble, working people, and many could not even gather the necessities of life. They were supported by the charity of Christians overseas, especially by the I.H.C.A., whom I represented in Israel.

The Jewish believers were diverse in their occupations, and also in their denominational convictions. There were Anglicans, Baptists, Pentecostals, and Plymouth Brethren, and many were not affiliated but just met in small groups in their homes reading the Word of God and praying for the salvation of Israel. All of them believe that the Lord Jesus is the Messiah and Savior and that He alone can meet all needs, including Israel's.

Will the Lord, through these "three hundred," save Israel? We pray that it might happen even as in the days of Gideon, as it is written:

> "And the LORD said unto Gideon, By the three hundred men . . . will I save you [Israel]" (Judges 7:7).

In August, 1964, we returned to the United States on furlough. I had gone to Israel alone, but returned with a wife and two children. Our marriage took place in Jerusalem on July 16, 1961. Estelle had found the Lord while taking refuge in a Baptist children's home outside Paris during Hitler's occupation of France. She was later baptized in a Jewish mission in Paris. She had come to Israel because she was convinced that her life as a Hebrew Christian would count more in this Jewish country. Our first baby, Judith Christine, was born at the Edinburgh Medical Mission Hospital in Nazareth, Israel. Our second baby was born in France while we stopped there on the way to the United States. Since there was an Rh blood factor, he was anemic for awhile. Before we returned to Israel, our third baby was born in the Presbyterian Hospital in Newark, New Jersey. Because of my health and educational problems, the I.H.C.A. had to appoint a younger man in my place. The door opened for us to remain in Newark to substitute for Rev. and Mrs. Isaac Finestone, who wanted to spend a sabbatical year in Israel.

Even before this year in Newark was over, a new door opened for us to come and teach subjects relating to Jews and Israel at Tennessee Temple Schools. Here also our fourth baby, Jonathan Roger, was born on April 4, 1968.

We continued living, working and witnessing to the Jewish community in Chattanooga and raising our four children. Soon the Lord closed this door, however, and opened a new door with the American Board of Missions to the Jews to work in Toronto, Ontario, Canada, in 1974. We worked there for nearly two years, ministering in churches and to the Jewish believers of that large city. At the time of this writing, our family resides in Cincinnati, Ohio, where I pastor a small congregation of mainly Jewish believers in the Messiah Jesus. The place is called *Kehilat Mashiach*, the Congregation of the Messiah. I serve on the executive committee of the Messianic Jewish Alliance of America (M.J.A.), to which position I was elected in 1975. I also edit the Messianic Jewish Quarterly (M.J.Q.) of this organization.

I still, of course, remain open to the Lord's leading, but I suppose that my direct ministry to the nation of Israel is over. Through my experience with that marvelous country whose existence is such a singular fulfillment of prophecy, I have made a few observations. Though Israel has greatly expanded her boundaries, the majority of the Jewish people still prefer to live outside the Promised Land. Yet

Israel is where Jewish history began and where, according to God's Word, it will be consummated.

Out of the pain and throes of World War II the state of Israel came into being and Jewish people are proud of her achievements. The hope of Israel to be a "light to the Gentiles" has not materialized. Many moral and previously friendly Gentiles have been disappointed with Israel's "wars of expansion," her failure to provide compensation to Arab refugees whose possessions Israel took over, and her failure to give full religious liberty and protection to the Hebrew Christians and missionaries. The only "light to the Gentiles" is still the Lord Jesus the Messiah. Jesus Christ is also part of the Jewish people. He is "the glory of His people Israel." One day Israel will also partake of this light and glory and then Israel's dream to be a light to the nations will be fulfilled. How shall these things happen, and when? The Hebrew Scriptures and the New Testament give us a clear answer. We read:

> And I will pour upon the House of David, and upon the inhabitants of Jerusalem, the spirit of grace and of supplications: and they shall look upon me whom they have pierced (Zech. 12:10).

In the New Testament we find how the great Hebrew scholar, the apostle Paul, describes this time when blindness shall depart from Israel:

> And so all Israel shall be saved: as it is written, There shall come out of Sion the Deliverer, and shall turn away ungodliness from Jacob (Rom. 11:26).

When this happens and Israel joins the Messiah, then will our people become a light to the whole world. Thus we will fulfill our age-long spiritual dream, as is foretold in God's Word:

Thus saith the Lord of hosts; In those days it shall come to pass, that ten men . . . shall take hold of the skirt of him that is a Jew, saying, We will go with you: for we have heard that God is with you (Zech. 8:23).

The apostle Paul adds:

Now if the fall of them be the riches of the world, and the diminishing of them the riches of the Gentiles; how much more their fulness? (Rom. 11:12).

My story is at an end now. It was written for the purpose of honoring and giving some account of the large group of Jewish believers in Europe, and especially in Poland, who perished. God would want their names remembered. Among them were giants of Jewish learning, like Yosele Sommer; giants of preaching, like Joseph Wolfin; giants in piety and dedication to God, like the Soffer family; and so many more.

It is also a tribute to those brethren who risked their lives to attempt to save a Jewish man, woman, or child. They did it altruistically because they loved their Lord Jesus better than their own lives. Only Jesus could inspire people to do it, so He must be the Messiah, Savior, Son of God. He was Jewish. Had our people received Him, this would not have happened. There is no doubt about it.

Let us search our ways and investigate our direction, and let us return to the Lord. There is no way of salvation without Him.

What a wonderful future there is to look forward to! I am confident that all the horrors that befell the Jews was simply the night before the Light will break for Israel and through her to the whole world.

For his anger endureth but a moment; in his favor is life: weeping may endure for a night, but joy cometh in the morning (Ps. 30:5).